BETWEEN TEACHER AND TEXT
Herbert Kohl, Series Editor

On the Side of the Child:
Summerhill Revisited

WILLIAM AYERS

Teacher with a Heart:
Reflections on Leonard Covello and Community

VITO PERRONE

ON THE SIDE OF THE CHILD

Summerhill Revisited

WILLIAM AYERS

Teachers College, Columbia University
New York and London

Published by Teachers College Press, 1234 Amsterdam Avenue, New York, NY 10027

Library of Congress Cataloging-in-Publication Data

Ayers, William, 1944-
   On the side of the child : Summerhill revisted / William Ayers
      p. cm. — (Between teacher and text)
   Includes bibliographical references
   ISBN 0-8077-4399-2 (paper : alk. paper) — ISBN 0-8077-4400-X (cloth :
   alk. paper)
      1. Summerhill School. 2. Neill, Alexander Sutherland, 1883-1973.
   I. Neill, Alexander Sutherland, 1883-1973. Summerhill. Selections. II. Title.
   III. Betweenteacher & text.
   LF795.L56A94 2003
   372.9426'4—dc21   2003055273

ISBN 0-8077-4399-2 (paper)
ISBN 0-8077-4400-X (cloth)

Printed on acid-free paper
Manufactured in the United States of America

10   09   08   07   06   05   04   03   8   7   6   5   4   3   2   1

Contents

SELECTIONS FROM
Summerhill: A Radical Approach to Child Rearing

A. S. NEILL

Series Foreword

Creative work does not spring forth fully formed from the effort of a single individual. It is always built on the previous work of others, on their efforts, mistakes, insights, and struggles. This holds as much for education as it does for music, dance, theater, physics, and mathematics. This series is an attempt to connect present educators with their predecessors through imaginary dialogs and personal narratives. It is a way of showing the minds of current educators at work at the same time as providing a personal way to enter the history of educational thinking and practice. The goal of the series is to illustrate to teachers and people who want to become teachers that there are living traditions that are transformed by current practitioners. Hopefully it can provide creative connections that will encourage teachers to consider themselves intellectuals and historians, and reaffirm the importance of the teacher as a creative force in the making of education.

The series is also meant to encourage educators to become actively engaged with ideas - not merely with techniques, methods, and strategies but with thinking about children, learning, and the place of education in creating a decent world. Thinking about education and reading past works in the field should not merely be a necessity imposed by taking classes at teacher education institutions. It should be a part of one's life as a teacher and hopefully some of these books will provide models of entering into a continuing and creative dialog with some of the most inspiring and challenging writing about learning and schooling.

I have asked a number of educators to choose a person whose work has been important to them and enter into dialog with that work and by extension with that person. I have also asked them to choose an excerpt from that text which has moved them. Each volume in this series has an essay by a current educator and a selection from the text they are reflecting on. In this way the hope is that you can get a flavor of the original as well as a feel for how it helps shape current thinking.

Paulo Freire, the Brazilian educator, often talked about "reading the word and reading the world." For him reading in both contexts implies entering into dialog. In the case of a text this dialogic reading consists, among other things, of questioning the text, relating it to one's active moral, political, philosophical and personal concerns. It can involve doubting the text, incorporating it into one's thinking or action, rewriting it for current times, fantasizing the author answering questions raised about it, and wrestling to give it current significance. It is an active, participatory experience that makes a text come alive in the present.

The books in this series are an attempt to do just this - to show the life in a text through its current transformations. The essays are not critical analyses of the texts, exposition of their ideas, or accounts of their historical or educational importance. Rather they are explorations of the texts and the lives of the authors, acts of discovery that can lead to new ways of thinking through current problems through the wisdom of past educational insights.

William Ayers' dialog with A. S. Neill, the founder of Summerhill and one of the great democratic educators of the last century, is particularly important at this time when high-stakes testing and an obsession with stigmatizing children as ADD or Hyperactive is a substitute for treating students as respected citizens of their schools. Neill and Ayers understand the importance of choice, voice, and respect in the lives of adolescents and they honor and celebrate it. It is important in these times, when people believe in controlling and scaring young people, and punishing them if they step out of the lines drawn by politicians and rigid educators, to hear democratic and loving voices. This book is an affirmation of what is strong about creative youth who reject conformity and about the educators who nurture their students' talents and skills so that they develop their critical sensibilities and use them well.

—Herbert Kohl, Series Editor

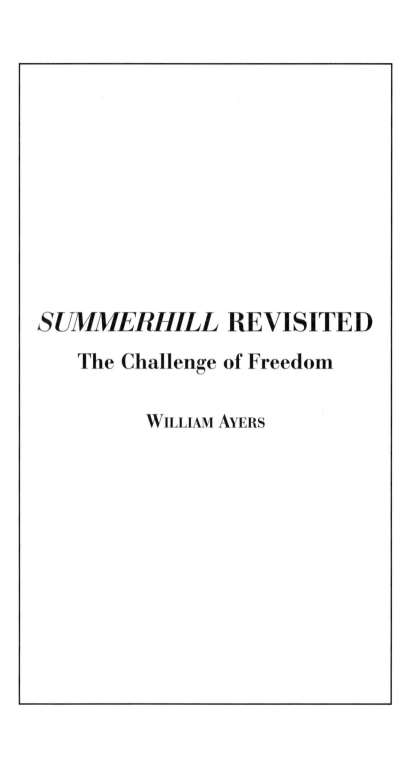

SUMMERHILL REVISITED

The Challenge of Freedom

WILLIAM AYERS

ONE

Love and Freedom

To Americans of a certain age, Summerhill is vaguely remembered as the radical experimental school from England where the kids made the rules, vanguard to the free school movement that swept the country in the 1960s. A. S. Neill, founder and director of the school, was a tall, stooped grandfatherly character, a Scotsman who looked a bit like John Calvin or Dr. Spock, take your pick. When I first learned of Neill and Summerhill I was sweating out my last days at Lake Forest Academy, a boarding school of the old type on Chicago's North Shore. Neill had just published the American edition of *Summerhill: A Radical Approach to Child Rearing*, and the reviews were clamorous. Some saw him as a pandering Pied Piper of sin and depravity, a naive fool or a dirty old man, the devil incarnate, while others said he was a prophet and a liberator. Similarly, Summerhill was pegged as either a little Gomorrah or a kind of Eden. One thing was crystal clear from the start: Neill and Summerhill had struck a powerful chord in the *zeitgeist* of the Sixties. For or against was a marker—it pointed to where you were likely to stand on every other critical issue of the day, and no one stayed neutral for long.

It's rather remarkable how odd things will occasionally collide and engage one another, taking on character and meaning in unexpected ways, for Summerhill was no more an idea of the Sixties than were sex, youthful upheaval, or rebellion. Neill founded Summerhill in 1921 when he was 37 years old and already well-known in England for his critical writings on education and child psychology. He'd been influenced by the revolution of Freud, by the juvenile prison reformer Homer Lane, and by Wilhelm Reich; he was in flight from his Calvinist upbringing and from the tyrannical rule of a cruel father.

Summerhill school was already 40 years old when I first encountered it, almost 45 by the time I began teaching and found suddenly indispensable Neill's vivid account of life at his little school. That was in 1965, and for me, as for so many others, Summerhill was a brilliant idea newly vitalized in a revolutionary age.

What captured me then, and what has the power to move me now, was Neill's seemingly bottomless commitment to children, his steadfastness and emotional generosity, and his willingness to take the side of the child even, or especially, when doing so seemed more than a little loony. The stories of his eccentric interactions with pupils became legendary: a boy was charged at General Meeting with destroying books in the library, and Neill proposed that he be appointed chief librarian; a girl was thought to be stealing money, and Neill gave her a few coins after each offense; Neill happened upon a couple of lads breaking windows with rocks and quickly joined in the mischief. In each case, according to Neill, the misbehavior disappeared almost instantly, providing further proof, if any were needed, that children flourished when they were accepted and encouraged to live their lives free of fear.

In these oft-told tales Neill can be rather easily discounted, for there's an innocence here—his apparent credulousness about simple psychological explanations, and his faith in the beneficence of humanity in a state of nature—as well as a sense of mild hectoring, as if he's hiding some of the evidence, marshalling his arguments for battle. But discounting Neill's ideas or the experience of Summerhill would be a mistake, for Neill was awakening to a revolution in thought in the early 20th century, a revolution shaking all the old foundations and laying the groundwork for the modern world: the rejection of superstition in favor of reason, the triumph of science, the positing of an unconscious in every human mind, the discovery of hidden laws in nature and in society that could be understood and mastered for the good of all. He broke with tradition, then, took the side of the *avante-guard* and the experimental, and created his daring school in the hope that his efforts might contribute to greater happiness in the world. For Neill, the principles guiding Summerhill were identical to the basic requirements for a healthy life, and they numbered two: love and freedom.

TWO

A Community of Children

I came to teaching from an odd direction beginning in 1965, as I've said, and the circumstances were these: I was a student at the University of Michigan, caught up in the civil rights struggle and the early stirrings of antiwar sentiment on the campus, and during the first international days of protest against the war in Vietnam I committed an act of civil disobedience, sitting in at the offices of the local draft board. Thirty-nine of us were charged with trespassing that day and carted off to county jail, and it was there that I heard about a freedom school in town from a fellow protester. Intrigued by his description of the place, I went to have a look as soon as I was released. What I found was enchanting and captivating, a little utopian dream called the Children's Community—they called themselves "an experiment in freedom and integration"—housed in a shabby church basement. The promise of the place pushed the sluminess to the side, and all I saw was color and laughter and life. I was hooked—I'd walked out of jail and into my first teaching job, and from that day until the present, teaching has been linked for me to the persistent longing for freedom, and the never-ending quest for justice.

I remember the buzz and hum of my first visit. There were dozens of separate things going on, nothing in lockstep, and it was impossible for me to take in more than impressions. There were books and paint and clay, posters of Frederick Douglass and Harriet Tubman on the walls, photos of Andrew Goodman, James Cheney, and Michael Schwerner. Several kids danced near a record player for a long time, and I remember two who seemed to do little more than run riot through the large room. I loved it.

The kids were sweet, of course, simply because kids are sweet, their wonder and vulnerability always combining to create a kind of special, spontaneous magic. Nothing shocked or even annoyed me—I carried inside of me my shaping experiences as the middle child in a large family. I knew noise and motion and the jumble of a community of kids close up.

Most days were like that first one—pockets of calm, eclectic projects and fleeting efforts in every corner, laughter and tears and a current of wildness that could ignite in a heartbeat, sending a rollicking handful of roughnecks harum-scarum around the room. I believed then—and I still do—that too many schools tried to break and control kids, enacting some cleaned-up kind of Calvinism, beating the hell out of them for their own good. I embraced wholeheartedly a contrary idea: kids are naturally good and will blossom beautifully if raised in freedom. A little Rousseau, a little Thoreau, a large dose of A. S. Neill and Summerhill. I never figured out how to adequately handle the wildest kids in their fullest eruptions—it didn't fit into my scheme of things, and I didn't know where to turn—so I mostly held on until the storm passed. I figured, as always, that eventually love itself would sort everything out. Love is a good starting point and a useful base to which to return. There's more, of course—much of it comes with experiences I'll describe further on—but this remains an essential compass.

We organized field trips to anywhere and everywhere: the bakery, the farmers' market, the Ford assembly line, Motown Records, the apple orchard. The Motown trip led to a book-making project based on our favorite singers, complete with song lyrics and autographed photos creating our own unique primers. The trip to the orchard led to a transformed school the next day: now it was a busy little bakery creating apple fritters and applesauce, apple pies, and apple muffins.

Experience, experience, experience. We wanted the kids to think, to be bold and adventurous, and so we pushed each other to be bold and adventurous as well, and to think ourselves. Trips became a big-letter statement about the centrality of first-hand experience as adventure and investigation and learning. Whenever a kid expressed an interest in anything—the weird, the bizarre, the intriguing, the surprising—off we'd go to have a look. We went to the hospital to visit a mother who worked as a nurse's aide, and to the county jail to visit Tony's uncle. We went to a dairy and followed the milk to market, then to a pork packing plant to trace the bacon—the strange little man in the bloody apron leading the tour was actually eating ribs. We went to the newborn nursery at the hospital, then to a funeral home and the county morgue. We didn't know how to stop or where. "Experience, experience," we said. Go further.

We had books in the Children's Community School—children's stories in Spanish and basal readers, hand-me-downs from garage sales and whole sets recycled from public schools. When one of the kids saw a book with black characters in it and remarked a little breathlessly that she hadn't known that there were books with black people in them, someone started a crusade. We bought every book we could find that featured black people—this was a Renaissance time in publishing African American authors of children's books—and we set up a book-making/publishing area in the school.

We bought a large-print primary typewriter for the kids, and used it to type stories the kids dictated, which they could illustrate themselves, or stories we made up about life in the school, featuring photographs of the kids and their adventures. Someone wrote a whole series about Jingles, our rabbit, that came out in monthly installments for a year. We cut pictures from newspapers and magazines and wrote stories around them. A favorite was *National Geographic*: Great pictures of kids and moms around which to spin mysteries and myths.

We had an ethic then of sacrifice and anarchy, and any contradictions to that ethic were largely ignored. The Children's Community paid room and board for all core staff, and our pay was twenty dollars a week. Of course we could afford it. We said that all kids were precious and innately good, and when some parents dropped really difficult kids with tough problems on us, we tended to gloss it all over and see it mainly as a test of our commitment. "All we need is love," we said. "The kids know everything," we said. I knew everything as a kid, but who cared? Pure myth, much of this, but we believed it wholeheartedly, and we tried to live it, too.

The Children's Community drew inspiration from several sources: the civil rights and peace movements; the contemporary critics of traditional school practice—John Holt, Paul Goodman, Jonathan Kozol, Jay Featherstone, Herb Kohl; the experimentalists—Caroline Pratt, Sylvia Ashton-Warner; and the old wise man himself, A. S. Neill. Neill was a standard reference for us, and *Summerhill* a text to mine for insight and direction, much as Dr. Spock's *Baby and Child Care* (also heavily influence by Freud and his followers) reassured generations of anxious parents to let their children be. Consult Spock on practically any issue and he begins, "Relax, that's just the natural way of babies," and with Neill something similar: "Possibly the greatest discovery we have made in Summerhill is that a child is born a sincere creature" (p. 126).* For Neill, freedom was the prerequisite to everything to come because "only under freedom can he grow in his natural way—the good way" (p. 125).

Love, then, as the starting point, and now freedom, a combination so hopeful in its affirmation of the humanizing potential of education, and so right in its rejection of authoritarianism, cruelty, domination, or hierarchy in the domain of childhood. "The difficult child is the child who is unhappy," Neill writes. "No happy man ever disturbed a meeting, or preached a war, or lynched a Negro" (1992, p. 7). He conflates the banal with the horrific and the apocalyptic here, but his point is straightforward: happiness is a necessary prerequisite for human solidarity, for fellow feeling. Sylvia Ashton-Warner, the renowned New

---

* Quoted material from *Summerhill: A Radical Approach to Child Rearing* is cited here with page numbers corresponding to the reprint of that volume as it appears in this book. References made to *Summerhill School: A New View of Childhood* appear with the year 1992 indicated, and page numbers correspond to that edition.

Zealand teacher, argues that a person is like a volcano with two vents—open the creative vent and the destructive vent atrophies and disappears; but if the creative side has no space or air or possibility of expression, the destructive will grow rapidly to monstrous, explosive proportions. The great Chicago poet Gwendolyn Brooks (1983) captures the same sentiment in two lines from her "Boy Breaking Glass": "I shall create! If not a note, a hole/If not an overture, a desecration."

A. S. Neill was often called "the man who loves children," but he objected:

> Love is hardly the word to use when a problem boy is breaking my school windows. One cannot love masses, only individuals, and not all individuals are lovable. No, I reject the word love; I prefer . . . "being on the side of the child," which means approval, sympathy, kindness, plus a complete absence of adult authority. It is of more value to understand children than to love them. (1992, p. 262)

By adult authority I take him to mean arbitrary or formal authority; moral authority is another matter, and it doesn't rely on structure for its power.

The link between happiness, confidence, fulfillment, and a more balanced social order seems both obvious to me and at the same time much more complex than Neill allows. He gets us started in a good place—there simply is no convincing argument for cruelty or repression or exploitation in the lives of children—and still there is more to do. As I said earlier, I draw from my first experience and my initial angle of regard—education at its best is linked to freedom and social justice. We start with love, on the side of the child.

THREE

The School in Society

When A. S. Neill and Ena Neill, his partner and lifelong collaborator, founded their "new kind of school" in the early 1920s they had one guiding idea: *"to make the school fit the child—* instead of making the child fit the school" (1992, p. 9). This idea contained within it a withering criticism of the status quo, the existing schools all around whose main business seemed, to the Neills at least, to be bending and breaking children, hammering them until they fit like cogs in a mindlessly menacing machine, automatons without the ability to think clearly or feel deeply. Why the steady focus on the curriculum, the lessons, the subjects? Why the obsession with punishment and reward, discipline and management, order and timetables? Why the forceful imposition of standardized ways of seeing and knowing? If the schools aimed to train a nation of sheep, the social implications were vast—violence, greed and exploitation unchecked, despotism, war, and fascism, "a society . . . carried on the shoulders of the scared little man" (1992, p. 15). Summerhill was set up, then, in the service of the resistance.

There are classrooms today consciously designed by thoughtful teachers to fit the child, and there are occasional schools where that describes the goal and the effort, but I cannot think of a single school system in the United States where anything remotely like it is either purpose or practice. Make the school fit the child—the words are as far-out and revolutionary today as when they were first uttered.

It's true that schools serve societies in all kinds of direct and indirect ways, that the schoolhouse is both window and mirror into any social order. This is easiest to see from a distance, and so, for example, if you'd wanted insight into the

11

workings of apartheid in the old South Africa, you could simply have peeked into the schools. You would have noticed white kids attending small classes with up-to-date equipment, and well-trained teachers dispensing a curriculum consistent with white supremacist assumptions; you'd also have seen black kids in overcrowded, collapsing buildings being fed a steady diet of obedience. Clearly one set of youngsters was destined for the mines and the mills, the fields and the prisons, while the other was being tutored to administer and profit from the injustice. Conversely, if you first knew the meaning of apartheid in general, you could have predicted what the schools would have had to look like in particular.

This relationship is true the world around. Think, for example, about the way Japanese children from early childhood onward are separated into vocational, professional, and intellectual tracks. Or why Israeli students are not allowed to read the internationally acclaimed Palestinian poet Mahmoud Darwish. Think what a country must look like if it denies an education to girls, or think of the larger purposes of a society that imposes a steep private tuition for a basic education on rich parents and poor parents alike. Think of one in which a traditionally excluded and oppressed ethnic minority makes up the majority in terms of school failure. All these things actually exist, and we can learn a lot about the goals and workings of any social order on earth by looking through the windows of its schools.

A. S. Neill's critique of U.S. schools was a broad one. In later writings he compared Soviet Russia and capitalist America, arguing that the "main difference between the two systems seems to be that one allows profit and the other doesn't. Both systems mould their children in home and school; both emphasize nationalism; both think that peace depends on the H-bomb; both inhibit the individual" (1992, p. 253).

The Soviet system has now passed away, but the criticism of our schools stands. In a broad sense our schools teach things like hierarchy and a child's place in it, indifference, emotional and intellectual dependency, provisional self-esteem, and the need to submit to certified authority. What, after all, is the lesson of report cards, grades, and the endless batteries of tests that play the part of autopsies rather than diagnostics? Don't trust yourself; seek approval from your betters.

And what is the point of the established schedule and the set periods (fifty minutes each for English, biology, study hall, P.E., and history), the exhaustive use of time, the uniform desks all in a row? You are not important; be malleable and productive in terms established by a higher authority. What is the point of all the elaborate surveillance, the locker searches and magnetic wands, the metal detectors and the complete lack of any private space? Imagination and privacy, so important to individual growth, are institutionally dangerous and therefore not tolerated.

Neill came to believe that the chief function of most schools is "to kill the life of children," to make them docile and obedient. "Would millions of free men allow themselves to be sacrificed to causes they had no interest in and did not understand?" he asked. "Is the future of humanity one of slaves ruled by an elite of powerful masters?" (1992, p. 259).

For many students the experience of schooling is easily summed up: Nothing of real importance is a part of classroom life, nothing is connected to anything else, nothing is pursued to its furthest limits, nothing is ever undertaken with investment or courage, and nothing of lasting value is ever accomplished. Too many schools seem, oddly, to celebrate ignorance, insisting that matters of real importance to students be banned as too controversial, or just plain diversionary, and that the present moment be worshipped as a point of arrival rather than as a complex and dynamic period like any other. Most schools fetishize rules, control, standardization, conformity, facts, and order, rather than honoring freedom, divergence, variation, creativity, novelty, flexibility, improvisation, and uniqueness. Most obsess about what Natalia Ginzberg (1989) has called "the little virtues"—things like thrift, caution, and a longing for material success—at the expense of the great virtues: generosity, courage, love, a desire to know and to be.

Few classrooms invite students to ask any serious questions: What's the evidence? How do we know? Whose viewpoint is privileged and whose left out? What are the alternatives, the connections, the resistances, the patterns, the causes? Where are things headed? Why? Who cares? It's no surprise, then, to find schools enveloped in a culture of complaint and cynicism, suffocating in a pervasive air of purposelessness, irrelevance, and fatalism.

In her novel *The Golden Notebook* Doris Lessing says it this way:

> It may be that there is no other way of educating people. Possibly, but I don't believe it. In the meantime it would be a help at least to describe things properly, to call things by their right names. Ideally, what should be said to every child, repeatedly, throughout his or her school life is something like this:
> "You are in the process of being indoctrinated. We have not yet evolved a system of education that is not a system of indoctrination. We are sorry, but it is the best we can do. What you are being taught here is an amalgam of current prejudice and the choices of this particular culture. The slightest look at history will show how impermanent these must be. You are being taught by people who have been able to accommodate themselves to a regime of thought laid down by their predecessors. It is a self-perpetuating system. Those of you who are more robust and individual than others, will be encouraged to leave and find ways of educating yourself—educating your own judgment. Those that stay must remember, always and all the time, that they are being moulded and patterned to fit into the narrow and particular needs of this particular society." (1962/1972, p. 17)

Our schools show us exactly who, as a culture, we are—the good, the bad, and the ugly—beneath the rhetoric and the self-congratulatory platitudes. If some of what we see is not as we would like it, well, we can search for all kinds of explanations and justifications; we can, in our defense, retreat to our good intentions; or we might conclude that some things *need* to be changed. We might even decide to join hands with others in order to create those changes.

Make the school fit the child—rather than forcing the child to fit the aspirations of anxious parents, the GNP or the military-industrial complex, some authorized lockstep course of study, or the existing hierarchies of race and class. Think about what a school fitted to the child might look like. Surely it would be generously supported, abundant with resources and materials of all kinds. It would be small, numbering no more than a few hundred students, so that participatory democracy could be enacted, practiced, and embodied. It would be a workshop for discovery and surprise, a laboratory for inquiry and experimentation. And the curriculum would unfold in endless pursuit of an inexhaustible question: What knowledge and experience is of most value?

Lessing's words echo Neill's earlier statements, and there's even more. For even in its own terms American education fails all students some of the time, and a large number of students all of the time. I'm pointing, of course, to the perennial problem of social class, and the dagger at the heart of the American experience: race.

FOUR

A Curriculum That Breathes

At Summerhill, "lessons are optional. Children can go to them or stay away from them—for years if they want to. There *is* a timetable—but only for teachers" (1992, p. 9). Neill is boasting a bit here; there's a swagger in his words. In reality kids at Summerhill wildly pursued projects and activities and perform-ances and, yes, lessons, too, which teachers prepared, developed, and delivered, but Neill is making a few points: children are learning all the time, and much of what they learn in traditional schools is to doubt themselves and to hate books; all children have an innate desire to learn and to grow and to become com-petent, which means that they will seek out the lessons they need when, and only when, they need them; there is nothing gained by trying to cram knowledge into the heads of putatively inert chil-dren—most will fail, some will resist, and a few of those who suc-ceed might well become mental giants and at the same time moral monsters. Feeling, emotion, heart—this is where it begins.

"Does ignorance matter?" Neill asked.

> They say that maths teaches one to reason, but I have yet to see a school staff room in which teachers rush to the maths man for advice. Most of us know nothing of zoology, botany, astronomy, mathematics, physics, philosophy. It is a fallacy that knowledge means power . . . Oscar Wilde wrote, "A cynic is one who knows the price of everything and the value of nothing." Often very knowledgeable men are anti-Semitic, using their knowledge to rationalize their hatred. It is no wonder that the masses distrust the intellectuals. (1992, p. 267)

Neill is again making a case for wholeness and for balance. "I am not saying knowledge is valueless," he writes. "The ideal is to know and to feel at the same time" (1992, p. 267). The whole child must somehow be held in view, the child of heart as well as head, the child of spirit and feeling and mind as well as body and brain.

Teachers often say, in effect, "I'm a teacher, not a social worker, a psychologist, a minister . . . ," but this is a fallacy. The fragmenting of children for the convenience of the balkanized and proliferating professions is a form of violence, and the splintering of specialties into finer and finer grades—getting nuttier and nuttier as they go along—means that we will no doubt some day have to invent a professional class to heal the split, to bring it all together somehow, just as we now talk of "integrated curriculum" as a bright new innovation when the original sin was segregating in the first place. There simply is no sensible, balanced, or peaceful way to cut the emotions of a child from the intellect, the heart or the spirit from the head. Each child is an unruly spark of meaning-making energy, dynamic, infused, connected, in motion. A teacher must also be a whole person, in motion and engaged with students who are themselves of a piece, and on a quest for meaning. "The function of the child is to live his own life . . . " (p. 79) says Neill, and we shouldn't ruin it from the start, for "youth is the time for ecstasy" (1992, p. 269).

I was talking about teaching in similar terms with someone who suddenly said to me, "But I think you have real disdain for content." Not at all, I replied. I sometimes feel the opposite, something like awe—or an obsession—for subject matters and materials, topics treated and the ways people make meanings. I seem to always have a half-dozen books begun by my bed, I rush to movies and plays, I stay up too late and get up too early—sometimes to read the *Science Times* or the *Arts*—all in the pursuit of "content." No, I said, I don't disdain "content" for a moment and I don't think Neill did, either, in his own life or the lives of his youngsters; what I disdain is the idea that content rules, that children are mere adjuncts and minor irritants to the content juggernaut. I object to an idea, apparent in classrooms everywhere, that treats it as obvious that each child in a group of youngsters should, or even could, get something of value at the same time in the same way in relation to the same stuff.

It's only recently in the long arc of human history—and only in some places—that teaching and learning has come to be conceived as something formal, structured, organized in a group. Most learning is in fact informal, experimental, slow, and idiosyncratic, like life in a family where kids imitate, mimic, imagine, play, and push in a largely safe place and in the company of a largely appreciative audience—the apprenticeship of full and responsible personhood. Neill saw Summerhill as a resistance to the sit-down-and-learn crowd and an affirmation of the natural instinct and disposition to learn that is every person's birthright.

I know it's silly to think that simply because it's 9 a.m. on October 15 every student in my class is eager or ready for the retreat to Dunkirk or the blitz of London, and why should they be? Frankly I can't think of a thing every child needs to know at the same time on the same day in the same way.

"That's ridiculous," my challenger said, returning to my presumptive disdain for content: "There are thousands of obvious things." I asked for an example, and he replied quickly, "Well, for example, every eighth grader ought to know the Bill of Rights." I felt myself begin to nod dully, automatically, but I caught myself and asked, "OK, what's the Seventh Amendment?"

To his credit he laughed and said, "I'm not an eighth grader." The point is not that knowing the Bill of Rights is unimportant. It's terribly important—perhaps particularly now that it's under such sustained attack—and so is reading history and literature, actively engaging with the arts, developing some scientific literacy, understanding current events, and being able to draw a map, say, of Afghanistan, Iraq, Saudi Arabia, Israel, Palestine, China, and more. But it's all in the service of something larger, something ineffable—wisdom, enlightenment, judgment, creativity, intellectual courage and engagement, freedom. These things can be nourished but not coerced, developed but not forced. Each is an accomplishment gained over time, each more likely to emerge in relationships and an environment vitalized by love, sustained through respect and acceptance, stimulated by both challenge and support.

Hannah Arendt captured this sense of larger purpose:

> Education is the point at which we decide whether we love the world enough to assume responsibility for it and by the same token save it from that ruin which, except for renewal, except for the coming of the new and the young, would be inevitable. And education, too, is where we decide whether we love our children enough not to expel them from our world and leave them to their own devices, nor to strike from their hands their chance of undertaking something new, something unforeseen by us, but to prepare them in advance for the task of renewing a common world. (1954, p. 196)

FIVE

The Child Becomes the Teacher

The first challenge of teaching—at once intellectual and ethical—is to see children and youth whole, as fully human, three-dimensional creatures with hopes and dreams and interests and skills that must somehow be taken into account. It's too easy to see their deficits and to miss their desires, to set off on a mission of righteous remediation without first embracing the aspirations or energies students might bring. Thinking only in terms of deficit and remediation is not a robust basis for building a school or a classroom. Our first steps must run toward understanding the child.

Teachers who accept this challenge are accepting an arduous pathway, and they quickly realize that they must begin by performing a kind of reversal: they need to become students of their students in order to become teachers of their students, and the dialectic is never linear—first this, then that—but always kaleidoscopic and dynamic, never finished. Good teachers observe and record, take in and reflect, stay still for a while, listen, research, and attend. They also act and interact, propose and perform, and then, back to observation, child-study, mini-ethnography, and action research. An endless circle—student/teacher, teachers/students. For the child is alive and moving, never summed-up, always on a journey, and so the teacher must be moving too, also on a quest, never a pat answer, never an authoritative summary of any child, each observation contingent, every conclusion tentative and written in disappearing ink.

What stands in the way of seeing the child? Everything—bell schedules and grades and tests and the press of time and schools that are too big, and classrooms too crowded. Perhaps most obtrusive is the toxic habit of labeling that infects our

schools top to bottom. "Behavior disordered," "educably mentally handicapped," L.D., T.A.G., and on and on into coded
incomprehension as we hear ourselves increasingly speaking a
half-language of credulousness that obliterates the living,
breathing child. Whatever is being described when we say, for
example, "behavior disordered (B.D.)," is never the whole story,
and yet that larger lived life is somehow eclipsed in the sticky
shadow of B.D. It stands in the way of a generous, compassionate, or hopeful vision, a true vision.

I was reminded of how nutty the labeling business has gotten by a headline in the *Onion*, a satirical newspaper that
describes itself as "America's greatest news source," that warns
of a growing epidemic among children: "An estimated 20 million U.S. children," it asserts, are believed to suffer from a "poorly understood neurological condition called YTD, or Youthful
Tendency Disorder." The article details the early warning signs
of YTD, including sudden episodes of shouting and singing,
conversations with imaginary friends, poor impulse control
with regard to sugared snacks, preferring playtime and flights
of fancy to schoolwork, and confusing oneself with animals and
objects like airplanes. An imaginary mother whose child was
recently diagnosed with YTD expresses relief: "At least we
know we weren't bad parents," she says hopefully. "We simply
had a child who was born with a medical disorder."

The satire works, of course, because it offers a cracked mirror of what is actually happening in our society. In and out of
school, children are the objects of this pervasive toxic barrage of
labels, stereotyped reductions of their humanity and their three-
dimensionality. Being young, it seems, is a pathology in need of
a cure.

Beneath some of the worst labels are assumptions that have
become the suffocating dogma of common sense. Think, for
example, of the wild popularity of *Lord of the Flies* and its encom-
passing view of the evil nature of children and childhood.
Shipwrecked and left to themselves, the kids turn into monsters
without the civilizing boot of the adult world.

Kenzaburo Oe, winner of the 1994 Nobel Prize for Literature, wrote his first novel, *Nip the Buds, Shoot the Kids* (1995) as a student, and it serves as an antidote to *Lord of the Flies*. In it he tells the story of a small band of juvenile delinquent boys evacuated during wartime to a remote mountain village where they are feared and hated by the superstitious and cruel inhabitants. The unnamed narrator—a boy who had been first sent to reformatory for stabbing a schoolmate, escaped, was recaptured, and sent again—describes a time "when maddened adults ran riot in the streets" and "there was a strange mania for locking up those with skin that was smooth all over, or with just a little glowing chestnut down; those who had committed petty offenses; including those simply judged to have criminal tendencies" (p. 26). When the fear of plague erupts, the villagers flee in the night, and the boys are cut off, abandoned, and barricaded inside the village to die. There, outside of time and in an autonomous space, the boys try to build a purposeful community of self-respect and love. The deaths of the narrator's brother and his brief lover prefigure the terror unleashed by the returning adults.

Locked in an outhouse, the boys are berated by the village headman, but after a string of threats, beatings, and humiliations, the villagers change their tack. Preparing for the return of the warden, they agree to let the crimes be bygones if the boys will tell a story of normalcy to the warden. When the narrator objects, the headman shouts him down: "Hey, who do you think you are? Someone like you isn't really human. You vermin can only pass on your bad blood. You'll be no good when you're grown up. . . . Listen, someone like you should be throttled while they're still a kid. We squash vermin while it's small . . . we nip the buds early" (pp. 185–186).

The narrator realizes no one will believe him anyway, that he holds no power in this world of adults who make the wars and also make the rules: "I was only a child, tired, insanely angry, tearful, shivering with cold and hunger." Banished in the night, forced to flee, he believes that "outside I would never be able to escape. Both inside and outside, tough fingers and rough arms were patiently waiting to squash and strangle me" (p. 188).

Oe goes through the looking glass, turning the *Lord of the Flies* on its head. His wrath is reserved for the adult world.

Oe captures something terrifyingly familiar about the predicament of youth today: the profound sense of alienation and disconnection, the vivid feeling of vulnerability at the hands of adults gone mad, the dark impression of being neither seen nor heard nor understood. It is a stark, frightening portrait.

What might it mean to respond to, instead of alienate, our children? Alejandro's voice, in Chris Carger's *Of Borders and Dreams*, asks,

> Right, a teacher shouldn't shove kids? Right, she shouldn't make fun of the way you talk? . . . She made a kid cry today. . . . I don't think it's right to make fun of somebody 'cause he doesn't know English. That's what she does sometimes. . . . Right, that's not good for a teacher to do? (1996, p. 42)

What can we learn from those who do respond to children's voices? Here is Haven Henderson's educator voice, grappling, in Mike Rose's *Possible Lives* (1995), with what multiple perspectives might mean for a teacher and for changing the structure of schools so that all students have the opportunity to learn as best they can:

> I'm going to be in a roomful of kids who think in lots of different ways about the world, and so do their parents. To think there's not that range of beliefs is ignorant. So is it fair for me to teach them only from the lens of my perspective? Or should I introduce many lenses? I think that's more powerful . . . to have a well-educated American population to challenge, to make democracy real, to teach kids that they can make a change happen, that they can be decision-makers, that they can make their communities better. That's our hope. (p. 235)

Or what might it mean to respond to Jonathan Kozol's devastating critique, in *Savage Inequalities* (1992), of the ways in which public schools are funded in the United States, and to the voice of Israel, a Puerto Rican boy at Morris High School in the South Bronx, who articulates the insidious effects of such inequalities:

> If you threw us all into some different place, some ugly land, and put white children in this building in our place this school would start to shine. No question. The parents would say: "This building sucks. It's ugly. Fix it up." They'd fix it fast—no question. People on the outside . . . many think that we don't know what it is like for other students, but we visit other schools and we have eyes and we have brains. You cannot hide the differences. You see it and compare. (p. 104)

In hearing these voices and others too long muted, can we dare to give up old ways of thinking, and reawaken the consciousness of possibility?

The center of the classroom must be the child—the work and activity of the child, the intentions and understandings of the child. While not the center, the teacher nonetheless has an awesome responsibility. For the child, this unruly spark of meaning-making energy at the heart of things carries two burning questions, mostly unstated and intuitive but still pervasive and always there: Who in the world am I? What in the world are my choices and my chances?

The aware and engaged teacher remembers the power of those questions for herself or himself, recognizes their urgency in the lives of all children, and turns to them again and again in everyday classroom interactions. Who in the world am I? is a question of personhood, of the individual in the crowd, of identity within multiplicity. What in the world are my choices and my chances? is a question of access and opportunity, of widening awarenesses, of texts and contexts. These are questions that drive the student; conscious of their power, they are questions that can drive the teacher as well.

"Hate breeds hate, and love breeds love," Neill said. "Love means approving of children and that is essential in any school.

You can't be on the side of children if you punish them and storm at them" (1992, p. 13). Neill found ways to separate the act from the person, an essential gesture if a child's humanity is of any concern. A hurtful or destructive act demands an immediate, spontaneous, personal, and authentic response, which makes it instructive. When the response is impersonal and bureaucratic the instructive quality is entirely lost.

Most education is incidental and informal, natural and inevitable. Classroom teachers might learn from games, plays, rites, traditions, and apprenticeships as they construct their environments for learning.

"I refuse to be classified as a teacher," Neill wrote. "Think what a tin god a teacher really is. He is the center of the picture; he commands and he is obeyed; he metes out justice; he does nearly all the talking" (1992, p. 101).

We may agree with Neill's contempt for the traditional, and still want to call ourselves teachers, or perhaps more accurately, people struggling to teach, on a journey toward teaching. It's a quest, after all, and a voyage, and as long as we are practitioners, no matter how long we've been at it and no matter how in-the-groove, we are always becoming teachers, and our basic rule, then, must be to reach. If after I'm gone someone were to say, "Oh, I remember Bill . . . he was a teacher," that would suit me fine. But until then I'm struggling, working, climbing my own pathway toward teaching.

Because teachers are whole people themselves, dynamic and diverse and driven to identity construction in the excruciatingly complex world of classroom and school, self-awareness, self-consciousness, and self-reflection are essential qualities to discover and nourish. It would be a mistake to go busily about trying to know your students while just as busily trying to hide from yourself. Self-knowledge is essential to teaching toward freedom.

SIX

Space to Grow

All true education is self-education, and everything else is sub-servience or servility. All real learning is characterized by dis-covery and surprise, the construction and reconstruction of meaning. Babies are by far the best learners, toddlers and young children quite good, because they are the least dogmatic. They push all five senses like sails toward the wind, every new, wild, unruly experience eagerly captured in order to propel them for-ward. "Childhood is playhood," says Neill, "and no child ever gets enough play" (1992, p. 32). He is thinking of imagination, fantasy, and imitation. "When a child has played enough," he continues, "he will start to work and face difficulties."

I remember my son Malik latching on to the word "ball" as an earlier signifier: Ball! Ball! Ball! As we walked up Broadway toward home at dusk, a rubber ball in his left hand, he would propulsively repeat the word, pointing to a grape, an apple, a sign, the moon. And in a matter of days, like magic, he changed his mind. "Moon," he said pointing to the face in the sky. There had been no intervening instruction, no lesson plan or remedial intervention, just life lived and sense made. The original classi-fication didn't hold; it was merely a convenient scaffolding to begin.

Others have imagined a world in which we teach "speak-ing" the way traditionalists teach "reading"—words would be broken into component parts to be taught separately; simple words like "a," "an," and "the" would be repeated until mas-tered; difficult words, "tyrannosaurus rex," for example, or "brontosaurus" or "giant" or "bulldozer" or "wrecking ball" or "Orion the Hunter" would be withheld until the middle years. Of course the result would be stupefying, and most of us would be rendered speechless. At that point the experts would arrive, diagnose a wide-ranging affliction, call it "disloquia," and the remedial clinical work would be up and running at full force.

As I write this it suddenly doesn't seem so far off or so far-fetched. If the pathologizing of ordinary life continues apace, if the pervasiveness of an engineering model for human development becomes much more widespread, and if education is further reduced by the imposition of a market metaphor—if all this goes on, then disloquia and worse loom just over the horizon.

But let's agree to resist it all, we teachers and educators, we parents and citizens and, yes, children and youth. Let's strike out in common cause for common sense and for humanity—for its enlightenment and liberation—all of us participants in the great adventure of being human, all of us trying to take a step toward understanding freedom.

Students can resist by refusing the pacifying stance of inert vessels to be filled up by all-knowing experts, deciding to demand an education, to seize one rather than to politely, passively receive one. And teachers can try to resist becoming monitors in a large sorting machine; they can take their students' lives seriously, attempt to challenge and nourish them in the same gesture, work and work and work on behalf of their students' growth and well-being.

Teaching is hard work, tougher than learning, because you must find an infinite number of ways to let students learn. And teaching is all that much tougher when you retreat from the spotlight, redirect the focus of attention to the students themselves, now at center stage. You place yourself to the side and become something new: the guide and the mentor, the coach and the conductor. You notice modes of energy everywhere, life and effort in a thousand directions. You need to summon new courage to teach in this place, a keener attentiveness, a more responsive style.

One new challenge will be to create an environment for learning and living that is rich enough, deep enough, and wide enough to embrace and challenge the students who actually walk through the door. It's not enough to have four walls and a roof; students must find possibilities to search and discover, to reach and accomplish.

The environment itself is a powerful teacher, something I first learned when I was a 20-year-old teacher and I took my kindergartners to watch the airplanes take off and land at the municipal airport. Everything seemed fine until we got to the mouth of the concourse, when everyone took off running as if at some prearranged signal, and I was haplessly pursuing them the length of the hall.

Next time we went I told them to hold hands with a partner, to stick together, to walk in an orderly manner to the end of the concourse where we would sit on a bench and I would reward them with snacks. They seemed to understand. But when we got to the top of that long, inviting hallway, BANG!, they were off as if my instruction meant nothing at all.

I learned something from all this—I learned that situations tell us what to do, and that the environment is a powerful teacher, so strong it trumps the lesson in almost every case. It made me want to attend more carefully to the classrooms I was creating, to question everything, to ask, for example, What kind of an atmosphere do I provide? What is the quality of experience students can create for themselves here? What techniques are available? Whose voices can be heard? What are the possibilities for ethical action?

It made me want to think hard about what materials invite discovery and surprise, what things open people to further learning. It made me more aware of what values were enacted, modeled, and demonstrated in my space. I've always wanted my classrooms to be kind places, welcoming places, places of thoughtfulness and compassion and participation, and I've wanted them brimming with books, magazines, and comics, with an author's corner and cozy spaces in which to read, and with walls bristling with student work. I've always wanted tons of paper and clay and sand, collage-making materials and wood and tools. I've always wanted food and recipes and a means to prepare meals together. All of this and more is in the service of children largely directing their own learning, of children actively engaging the questions of identity and access.

I'm reminded of a passage from Doris Lessing's autobiography, *Under My Skin*. By the age of 12, she says, she knew:

> how to set a hen, look after chickens and rabbits, worm dogs and cats, pan for gold, take samples from reefs, cook, sew, use the milk separator and churn butter, go down a mine shaft in a bucket, make cream cheese and ginger beer, paint stenciled patterns on materials, make papier-mâché, walk on stilts, . . . drive the car, shoot pigeons and guineafowl for the pot, preserve eggs—and a lot else . . .
>
> That is real happiness, a child's happiness: being enabled to do and to make, above all to know you are contributing to the family, you are valuable and valued. (1994, p. 103)

To do and to make, to know you are valuable and valued. Who in the world am I? What in the world are my choices and my chances? Here is where teaching begins. Here is where freedom takes hold.

SEVEN

Little Is Beautiful

Summerhill was established to be "on the side of the child," which to Neill meant "abolishing all punishment and fear and external discipline; it meant trusting children to grow in their own way without any pressure from outside, save that of communal self-government" (1992, pp. 208–209). Neill thought that freedom itself would be a hollow farce without children having the formal ability and the power to govern their own social lives. Democracy was the rule, freedom the goal.

Neill acknowledged that children learn the difference between freedom and license rather slowly, but they can know right away that they are loved. "In Summerhill, there is one perennial problem that can never be solved; it might be called the problem of *the individual v. the community*" (pp. 97–98).

Neill made a necessary distinction between freedom and license. He said that students occasionally arrived at Summerhill with the attitude, "This is a free school, I'll do what I like. . . . It took them some time to grasp the fact that freedom does not mean doing exactly as you like. They found that in a self-governing school they had to obey the laws made by the whole community" (1992, pp. 257–258).

Neill described himself as pro-democracy, plain and simple, but beyond that, apolitical, even antipolitical:

> All my life I could never catch crowd emotion. I could never wave a flag, shout a slogan, never become active in any party, political or otherwise. A rank individualist dealing with a crowd of kids. . . . My politics, happily, are mostly confined to our school democracy, which is as near real democracy as it can be. We meet in a big room and make our laws by general show of hands. (1992, p. 256)

His true politics were the politics of participatory democracy, a politics of the small town or the village square, a face-to-face politics suited to youngsters and oldsters alike.

Participatory democracy is a useful concept around which to create classroom life, for it is a large idea with myriad practical implications, and it points unwaveringly toward the social and the ethical. Traditional teachers are taught, in effect, that social and ethical matters dwell in a separate realm from cognitive or intellectual things. "Classroom management" or "school discipline"—the obsession of most new teachers, and for good reason: the kids outnumber us thirty or so to one, and they don't even want to be there—is assumed to be a set of skills to be mastered and employed *in order to teach*. In other words, the relentless message is this: first, get control; then, teach the stuff.

The problems with this approach are legion. For example, it assumes that "get control" is neutral and without powerful lessons of its own embedded right at its heart. If children are learning all the time, and if what they are learning isn't necessarily stipulated nor intended by us, the "get control" regimen could simultaneously teach things like authoritarianism, power as the basis of respect, avoidance, postponement, falseness, cynicism, and fatalism. Students may display submission and comportment while learning to feign interest and industry, all the time being bored out of their minds, disconnected, possibly storming.

Further, external control is always weak and slippery, and "control" in any final sense is elusive—it's not a state, established and complete, something finished once and for all. This one-dimensional concept creates a deep sense of defeat and failure in most teachers because problems just keep cropping up.

A healthier stance, the participatory democracy approach, assumes that people ought to make the decisions that effect their lives, and that it's never too soon (and usually not soon enough) to begin practicing judgment and decision-making. In fact no one is wise before being innocent, experienced before inexperienced, and so if a democratic society is our ideal, it make sense to practice democracy right from the start.

For teachers there's a dimension that makes participatory classrooms not only richer and more meaningful, but more practical as well. This is because, ideally, control is not external and exclusive, concentrated in a single tentative grip, but is internal to the group, shared equally by everyone. This means that *learning to live together* is on the agenda every minute of every day; *learning to live together* is the assumed curriculum regardless of whatever else is being considered or pursued; *learning to live together* collectively, associatively, is a challenge our whole lives through.

So many "behavior problems" in classrooms are created directly and explicitly by school policy and by teachers. I remember visiting a kindergarten class in Chicago where the teacher pronounced the little ones "incorrigible"—she had each at a desk for hours on end completing little work sheets, squirming, fidgeting, and behaving exactly like the 5-year-olds they were, which was, in this tyranny, misbehaving. If students of any age are engaged in inappropriate or meaningless and purposeless activity hour after hour, day after day, it's a wonder they don't rebel more often and more forcefully. In any case, in those places there's a logic to the language of warfare and prison camps—"in the trenches," "on the front lines," "lockdown," "search and seize."

In the cafeteria of a neighboring high school—a school with metal detectors, hidden cameras, and regular locker searches—I read the "RULES," written in large block letters and posted high above the entrance: NO RUNNING, NO LOUD TALKING, NO THROWING FOOD, NO FORK FIGHTS . . . No fork fights? There were a few more "NOs" but that fourth one really got my attention. What weird or horrid event, I wondered, occurred in the long ago that led to that fourth rule? There was nothing, after all, posted about knife fights, fist fights, or gun fights— only fork fights. How strange. And horrible.

Listing the rules as a series of "NOs" makes some sense— it acknowledges that people are here against their will and desire, that the potential for chaos is great, and that a higher authority has the power and the will to press its demands upon you, sensible or not, like it or not. But the practical problems are also large: no list, no matter how long, could contain every possible hurt or harm, every conceivable mischief or annoyance; your imagination (and mine) is inadequate to catalogue the possible offenses—fork fights?—and the entire regimen casts a pall on the world of the young, a world that might be hopeful and optimistic and bright if we began somewhere else.

"Love is being on the side of the other person," (1992, p. 55) Neill argued. Love begins in approval.

Where to begin? One of my favorite teachers gathers the fifth graders in a circle on the first day and tells them that there are three classroom rules: (1) you *can* chew gum in class, but not in the larger school where it's outlawed, (2) you *can* wear hats in class ("I can read and do my work wearing a hat, so I assume you can, too") but not in the school where "NO HATS!" is fiercely enforced—at this point the kids are wildly enthusiastic about fifth grade—and (3) because this is a learning community, we all have to learn to live together with respect.

The rest of the morning is a wide-ranging conversation that begins to fill in the meanings, the gaps and wide-open spaces in rule number three. A process of standard-setting is underway, a process that will unwind for the whole year, take on complexity, density, and weight as it goes along. *How shall we live together? What is all this living about?* Teachable moments will surface unexpectedly—Jason took Dan's calculator without asking, a group of kids begins teasing a clumsy classmate, some boys decide to exclude girls from an activity—and each will be the occasion for more sophisticated understandings and behaviors.

I'm reminded of an episode in E. B. White's delightful odyssey of a clever mouse, *Stuart Little* (1945), when the protagonist arrives in a small town early one morning and sees a troubled man sitting on the curb. When Stuart inquires, the man explains he's facing an "impossible situation" because he's the local superintendent of schools. "That's not an impossible situation," Stuart replies sympathetically. "It's bad, but it's not impossible." (p. 84).

The superintendent tells Stuart that one of his teachers is ill and he can't find a substitute. Stuart volunteers to stand in for the day; the superintendent is relieved, but immediately wary, wondering if Stuart can maintain discipline. "Of course I can," Stuart says confidently. "I'll make the work interesting and the discipline will take care of itself" (pp 86–87).

E. B. White is skewering schooling as we know and practice it. We can see Stuart as a kind of A. S. Neill character: eccentric, eclectic, irreverent, and charismatic. He's a clever mouse after all, full of common sense and more than a bit the rebel. Climbing up to the desk hand-over-hand on a yardstick and jumping from a stack of books onto the bell to get their attention, Stuart addresses the class. Once he determines no one is either late or absent, he leaps into a conversation about what they ordinarily do—we'd call it "curriculum."

A typical morning, the students tell their neat little substitute, is broken into the following subjects: arithmetic ("Bother arithmetic!" Stuart snaps. "Let's skip it"); spelling (Stuart finds misspelled words "an abomination" and urges his young charges to consult a dictionary regularly); writing; and social studies ("Social studies?" Stuart asks, incredulous. "Never heard of them.")

Stuart suggests that on this morning they talk about what's really important, and asks if the students know what that is. One student offers "a note in music" and "the way the back of a baby's neck smells;" another, "ice cream with chocolate sauce on it" (p. 92). When the conversation turns to rules and laws, the dialogue could be in the meeting room at Summerhill: A student suggests a good law might be to never poison anything but rats, but Stuart argues a law has to be fair to everyone, and the poison law wouldn't be fair to rats. He maintains that rats are underprivileged, and if everyone would just stop persecuting them, rats might come out in the open more often and learn to get along better with others. The conversation rambles along like this through the whole day, circling back to what's really important, what's fair, and how we can get along.

The class reaches a consensus, of sorts, that an essential rule is "absolutely no being mean" (p. 94). E. B. White's Stuart Little is a critic of the mindless and the cruel in school; he's the cheerful, charismatic creator of a classroom that engages children's energies and imaginations. Stuart is like a mousy Neill—full of generous good humor, innocence, fellow feeling, a bit of anarchy, and a love of freedom. He's on the side of the child.

EIGHT

Democratic Vistas, Moral Action

Neill's concern was for the lives of his own contemporary children, as well as the children of coming generations and for a future in which the public could no longer summon its courage or its initiative or its authority precisely because the youth had lost the capacity for free thought or deep feeling. He felt "the world has become more sinister, more dangerous, and here I am not thinking of wars, I am thinking of the diminishing power of the people and the growing power of the big businesses, the combines, the dehumanization of industry" (1992, p. 244).

Myles Horton, founder of the Highlander Folk School, a central site of civil rights education and organizing in the South in the 1950s and 1960s, had a straightforward view of democracy that echoed in many ways Neill's common sense stance:

> To arrive at democratic decisions, you need to have a bunch of ordinary people sitting around the stove in a country house or store and contributing their own experience and beliefs to the discussion of the subject at hand. . . . Then you take a poll of the majority of those present, regardless of who they are, and that is a democratic decision.

To build democratic schools is to work toward a democratic future, recognizing that democracy is always a community in the making, always an aspiration we approach fitfully. The soul of democracy is a social spirit of compassionate solidarity, of engagement, of sympathy, empathy, and connectedness. It begins in care and cooperation, and the recognition that our lives are suspended in interdependent webs of relationship. That spirit can never be achieved by reference to forms and procedures alone, but rather is fueled by a sense that injustices can be opposed and justice aspired to, that questions can remain open to dialogue and debate, that people can develop the ethical knowledge to stand up and count for something, and that human beings can learn to live together in common cause. All of this is a possibility, neither certain nor necessarily probable, but something to imagine and pursue.

Education can strengthen the capacity to act for the common good and to take risks on behalf of a moral vision, but only insofar as ideas about democracy and morality become part of the lived experience of young people. John Dewey championed the basic idea that school should not be thought of as preparation for life, but as life itself, and that the only way to prepare for a democratic life is to live a democratic life. In the absence of that, all the reenactments of the foundational speeches, the memorization of the early texts, the recitation of pledges and the saluting of flags are worse than empty gestures—they become obstacles to the realization of democracy.

People too often operate schools as if children's sole function in life is to serve the needs of others, ultimately of large impersonal corporations and the military, as if the only role anyone will ever play in life is functionary, follower, consumer. How else to explain all the policing and flattening aspects of school routine, all the obsessive leaping on misbehavior as if the principle of moral action is rule-following? A more inspiring goal is to hope for each child the opportunity to become a productive citizen, a community participant, a responsible family member, a good neighbor, a producer, an appropriate leader. All roles and relationships are important, and none comes to a person full-blown and ready-made. The habit of democratic living and moral action is in the doing.

Moral action is about more than individual behavior; it's also about questioning and engaging the world we live in: Do we live in a moral culture or an ethical community? How do we behave as a group? How does our society act?

Community ethics takes note of the fact that most people act within the norms of the society they inhabit—most Trojans act like Trojans, most Romans like Romans—and looks, then, to common goals and collective problems, the laws we pass and the choices we make as a group. We know that a slave society undermines goodness every moment in a million different ways, and that the slave owner who pays his bills or the honest overseer are not models of moral behavior. Because it is nearly impossible to live a virtuous life in a slave state, it becomes essential to end slavery. Working toward a more just society creates the conditions for more of us to act more often in a moral way.

Education is always an arena of hope and struggle: hope for a future with a widened set of possibilities; and struggle over access and equity, quality and content. Education is a space where people come together to name and enact what they want for themselves and their children and society, and what obstacles they hope to overcome. Education is where we decide what is most worthwhile to know and experience, and how to get there. It's no wonder, then, that education is often a field of conflict.

We are suffering at this moment both a dramatic retreat from the great humanizing mission of education and the relentless embrace of criminal justice as the solution to every problem we face. Massive prison construction replaces school construction; school budgets are cut while military and police budgets balloon; more black American men encounter the justice system than the university system; and criminalizing language becomes commonplace in schools: three-strikes-and-you're-out, discipline and punish, zero tolerance.

The cultural policy of zero tolerance is a knife in the heart of education. Education extends opportunities and makes connections. Education opens minds and opens doors. Education is relational—its tone, intimate; its basic gesture, an embrace; its discourse, dialogue. Education demands assent, participation, and reexamination.

Zero tolerance is exclusionary and intolerant, and it signifies the end of dialogue, reflection, intimacy, relationship. Zero tolerance is characterized by a casting out, and it represents, therefore, the end of education as a relentlessly humanizing enterprise, and the triumph of a narrow, authoritarian view of children and youth.

Rather than allow the putative demands of the larger social order dictate life in schools, we can perhaps imagine taking the young child in a loving and vital environment, a "trickle-up" model that might impact the upper grades, the high school, colleges and universities, and the social fabric as a whole. We might take the side of the child, and in so doing, we might be rewarded with a better vision of a good world.

NINE

Unfreedom

What is this thing called freedom? What does it mean in the lives of individuals, of schools, of whole societies? In what way is it imaginable or achievable? Does it matter?

Neill wrote toward the end of his life that he felt a deep pessimism about the "slow growth of freedom. . . . Have we time to bring up children who will be free emotionally? Free from hate and aggression, free to live and let others live?" (1992, p. 248). For Neill, freedom was fairly simple and straightforward—to live and to let live—and fundamentally linked to psychological well-being—"the child free from inhibitions, the parents free from neurosis" (1992, p. 250).

Who could object? These are nice-sounding words, hopeful goals. On the other hand, where do they leave us? The realm of Neill's concerns is important to me, critical in fact, and is neglected at our peril. But there is more. Let me sketch some other necessary dimensions of the discussion of freedom and education.

Talk of freedom is pervasive in every realm—free trade, the free world, free markets, free exchange—but it feels oddly abstract, a given that is both ubiquitous and distant, assumed but not available for active or concrete participation. Personal freedom—our vaunted rights and choices, our assumed autonomy and insistent independence—is similarly saturating but perversely elusive: free to drive anywhere, we find ourselves stuck in traffic; free to speak our minds, we don't have much to say; free to choose, we feel oddly entangled; free to vote for the candidate of our choice, we can't find anything distinctive about either.

Most of us, of course, are also entirely dependent on others for a living—we have no voice and no vote in what will be pro-

duced or how. Most of us experience the flattening and pacifying effects of a mass consumer society—the sense of being
manipulated, lied to, shaped and used by powerful forces. We
hear all around us market fundamentalists promoting the idea
that the purest forms of freedom and choice and democratic living can be easily reduced to a question of consumption. Many
Americans seem to assume that freedom requires neither
thought nor effort—we lucky few were somehow simply born
free, it's our inherited state. But for all human beings there is the
condition of being, in Hannah Arendt's phrase, "free and fated,
fated and free" (1963, p. 33). We are not entirely determined, but
neither do we enjoy absolute choice. None of us chooses our
parents, for example, or our historical moment; no one chooses
a nation or tribe or religion to be born into. We are thrust into a
world not of our choosing. On the other hand each of us chooses who to be against a hard background of inherited facts. In
some situations we might accede, in others, refuse. Like everyone we are situated; we are on our own, free and fated. When
freedom is abstractly and easily proclaimed—whether in school
or society—we should proceed as skeptics.

Further, freedom as an individual attribute has an arid and
incomplete quality to it. It lacks both the sense of accomplishment—freedom as something achieved through conscious
choice, through active pursuit—and the sense of solidarity, the
understanding that human beings are linked to one another by a
thousand threads and that isolation can never be synonymous
with freedom. Janice Joplin's "Freedom's just another word for
nothing left to lose" leaves us suspended in a solipsistic vacuum.

The Chinese ideograph representing people is called *ren*,
and is made up of two leaning strokes, each supporting the
other. It looks as if, should you remove one, the other would col-
lapse. How might we think of associative freedom, of freedom
with rather than from others, of freedom in ways that engage,
energize, and activate a community?

Hannah Arendt describes a freedom involving "participation in public affairs, or admission to the public realm" (1963, p.

32). She acknowledges that freedom involves the establishment of certain rights within a domain of privacy, spaces where people are neither coerced nor obstructed, but she argues that this in itself is a rather narrow and negative approach to freedom, that the domain of the personal and the private is not the "actual content of freedom." The content of freedom is found, rather, in "a body politic"; that is, in those public spaces where people come together freely as authentic beings to name the obstacles to their own humanity: "a body politic which is the result of covenant and 'combination' becomes the very source of power for each individual person who outside the constitutional political realm remains impotent" (p. 171).

Arendt describes the American revolution as an event "made by men in common deliberation and on the strength of mutual pledges. The principle which came to light during those fateful years . . . was the interconnected principle of mutual promise and common deliberation" (1963, pp. 213–214). And this "principle which came to light" also drove the French and the Haitian revolutions, the German, the Russian, and the Chinese revolutions, the movements in Hungary in 1956 and Poland in 1979. In each case, in a time of crisis and change, citizens came together spontaneously—whether in town meetings, communes, workers' councils and soldiers' committees, or soviets—in order to create a public space for the expression of their dreams and their demands. It was in these public spaces that, according to Arendt, freedom came to life, and she referred to them as "treasures," for they embodied the "hope for transformation of the state, for a new form of government that would permit every member of the modern egalitarian society to become a 'participator' in public affairs. . . . " It was this treasure "that was buried in the disasters of twentieth-century revolutions" (pp. 264–265), destroyed and murdered by foreign invasions and occupations, and by elites and vanguards from all sides. It remains, for Arendt and for others, the "lost treasure" central to the modern predicament.

Freedom is linked for Arendt to a space for human interaction. She argues that authentic political action requires this free space, created and sustained by people coming together. This is distinct from a personal, private, or inner *feeling* of freedom, something that can be achieved through escape or retreat or isolation—through drugs, to take the most obvious example.

Schools are sites of hope and struggle, an obvious venue for the creation of a public space, the space of freedom. People are coming together, searching for something better, deciding what we value, what we hope to pass on, who we want to be, and how we want to create the new. For those of us who hope for a more robust and vital sense of freedom, schools must become places where the soul of democracy is brought more fully to life. This means, among other things, that a spirit of mutuality and human solidarity, of connectedness and commonality, pervades both the culture and the curriculum. Dialogue—the back and forth based on the possibility of changing others and at the same time your self being changed—becomes the emblematic method. The three Rs are transformed, then, as a dazzling Chicago teacher named Liz Kirby has proposed in her school, into Relevant, Rigorous, and Revolutionary. At its best education is engaged and engaging, demanding and serious, and full of the propulsive energy to transform.

I argued earlier that a primary challenge to teachers is to see each student as a three-dimensional creature—a person much like themselves—with hopes, dreams, aspirations, skills, and capacities; with a body and a mind and a heart and a spirit; with experience, history, a past, a pathway, a future. This knotty challenge demands sustained focus, intelligent judgment, inquiry and investigation. It requires wide-awakeness since every judgment is contingent, every view partial, every conclusion tentative. The student is dynamic, alive, in motion. Nothing is settled, once and for all. No view is all views and no perspective is every perspective. The student grows and changes—yesterday's need is forgotten, today's claim is all-encompassing and brand new. This, then, is an intellectual task of serious and huge proportion.

As difficult as this challenge is, it is made tougher and more intense because teachers typically work in hierarchical

institutions of power and control, where the toxic habit of labeling kids by their deficits has become commonplace. The language of schools is too often a language of labeling, a language
of reduction, a language lacking spark, dynamism, imagination,
or the possibility of freedom. Whatever the labels point to—
even when glimpsing a chunk of reality—is reductive and
overdetermined in schools. In this way they represent un-free-
dom: repression, coercion, entanglement. The thinking teacher
needs to look beneath and beyond the labels, to reach toward
freedom.

Schools both serve and mirror the larger social order. While
they are established to recreate the norms and values of society,
schools are also sites of contention, reflecting, for example, long-
term struggles and conflicts between democratic impulses and
oppressive relationships. To justify or recommend a society's
schools, one must be able to somehow warrant the society. The
"failure" of black schools in the old South Africa, as noted earlier, was really no failure at all. It fit at least some of the overar-
ching needs and goals of South African society. However, South
Africa's schools were also a key source of the liberation movement, the place where liberating ideas were learned and sometimes even practiced. The sustained struggle of South African
militants arose from the schools, and schools were both site and
seedbed for the liberation struggle.

A similar argument can be made here at home: the failure
of some schools and some children in Chicago, say, is not due to
a failure of the system. If we suspend for a moment the rhetoric
of democratic participation, fairness, justice, and freedom, and
acknowledge (even tentatively) that our society, too, is one of
privilege and oppression, inequality, class divisions, and racial
and gender stratifications, then we might view the schools as a
whole as doing an adequate job both of sorting youngsters for
various roles in society and convincing them that they, and they
alone, deserve their various privileges and failures. Sorting students may be the single, brutal, and abominable accomplishment of U.S. schools, even if it runs counter to the ideal of edu-

cation as a process that opens possibilities, provides opportunities to challenge and change fate, and empowers people to control their own lives. Nowhere is this contradiction more visible than in the experience of poor and black children and youth in American schools.

Speaking of the educational "strategies of failure" a generation ago, Annie Stein (1971) concluded:

> This is a massive accomplishment. . . . It took the effort of . . . teachers, administrators, scholars, and social scientists, and the expenditure of billions to achieve. Alone, however, the "professional" educators could not have done it. They needed the active support of all the forces of business, real estate interests, trade unions, willing politicians, city officials, the police, and the courts. . . . Perhaps an even greater achievement of the schools has been their ability to place the responsibility for this extraordinary record of failure upon the children themselves, their families, and their communities. Social scientists engage in learned disputes as to whether it is heredity or environment that makes the child of poverty an inferior form of humankind—but the assumption of his inferiority is not disputed, except by his parents and by the child himself. (p. 159)

"Does the Negro need separate schools?" W.E.B. DuBois asked in 1935, commenting on the dreadful miseducation black children suffered in America. "God knows he does. But what he needs more than separate schools is a firm and unshakable belief that twelve million American Negroes have the inborn capacity to accomplish just as much [as] any nation of twelve million anywhere in the world ever accomplished, and that this is not because they are Negroes but because they are human" (2002, p. 140). DuBois went on:

> I know that this article will forthwith be interpreted by certain illiterate "nitwits" as a plea for segregated Negro schools and colleges. It is not. It is simply calling a spade a spade. It is saying in plain English: that a separate Negro school, where children are treated like human beings,

trained by teachers of their own race, who know what it means to be black in the year of salvation 1935, is infinitely better than making our boys and girls doormats to be spit and trampled upon and lied to by ignorant social climbers, whose sole claim to superiority is the ability to kick "niggers" when they are down. I say, too, that certain studies and discipline necessary to Negroes can seldom be found in white schools.

It means this, and nothing more.

To sum up this: theoretically, the Negro needs neither segregated schools nor mixed schools. What he needs is Education . . . there is no magic, either in mixed schools or in segregated schools. A mixed school with poor and unsympathetic teachers, with hostile public opinion, and no teaching of truth concerning black folk, is bad. A segregated school with ignorant placeholders, inadequate equipment, poor salaries, and wretched housing, is equally bad. Other things being equal, the mixed school is the broader, more natural basis for the education of all youth. It gives wider contacts; it inspires greater self-confidence; and suppresses the inferiority complex. But other things seldom are equal, and in that case, Sympathy, Knowledge, and the Truth, outweigh all that the mixed school can offer. (p. 143)

Neill asked, "How can we have happy homes with love in them when the home is a tiny corner of a homeland that shows hate socially in a hundred ways?" (1992, p. 250). For Neill love and freedom were forever bound together, and so we might ask, Can we really be free in a corner of the room if unfreedom pervades the rest of the house?

TEN

Freedom and Revolution

Good teachers must know and care about some aspect of our shared life—our calling, after all, is to shepherd and enable the callings of others. We need to stay wide awake to the world, to the concentric circles of context in which we live and work. Teachers, then, invite students to become somehow more capable, more thoughtful and powerful in their choices, more engaged in a culture and a civilization. More free. How do we warrant that invitation? How do we understand this culture and civilization?

Teachers choose—they choose how to see the world, what to embrace and what to reject, whether to support or resist this or that directive. As teachers choose, the ethical emerges. James Baldwin (1996) states that:

> The paradox of education is precisely this—that as one begins to become conscious one begins to examine the society in which he is being educated. The purpose of education, finally, is to create in a person the ability to look at the world for himself, to make his own decisions, to say to himself this is black or this is white, to decide for himself whether there is a God in heaven or not. To ask questions of the universe, and then learn to live with those questions, is the way he achieves his own identity. But no society is really anxious to have that kind of person around. What societies really, ideally, want is a citizenry which will simply obey the rules of society. If a society succeeds in this, that society is about to perish. The obligation of anyone who thinks of himself as responsible is to examine society and try to change it and to fight it—at no matter what risk. This is the only hope society has. This is the only way societies change. (pp. 219–220)

Teachers are the midwives of hope or the purveyors of determinism and despair. In *Beloved*, Toni Morrison's novel of slavery, freedom, and the complexities of a mother's love, Schoolteacher, a frightening character with no other name, comes to Sweet Home with his efficient, scientific interest in slaves and makes life unbearable for the people there. Schoolteacher is a disturbing, jarring character for those of us who want to think of teachers as caring and compassionate people. Schoolteacher is cold, sadistic, brutal. He is all about control and management and maintaining the status quo. He and others like him are significant props in an entire system of dehumanization, oppression, and exploitation. They show us teaching as unfreedom, teaching as linked to slavery.

Toward the end of Amir Maalouf's *Samarkand*, a historical novel of the life of Omar Khayam and the journey of *The Rubaiyat*, Howard Baskerville, a British schoolteacher in the city of Tabriz in old Persia at the time of the first democratic revolution, explains an incident in which he was observed weeping in the marketplace: "Crying is not a recipe for anything," he begins, "nor is it a skill. It is simply a naked, naive and pathetic gesture" (Maalouf, 1994, p. 234). But, he goes on, crying is nonetheless important. When the people saw him crying they figured he "had thrown off the sovereign indifference of a foreigner," and at that moment they could come to Baskerville "to tell me confidentially that crying serves no purpose and that Persia does not need any extra mourners and that the best I could do would be to provide the children of Tabriz with an adequate education" (p. 234). "If they had not seen me crying," Baskerville concludes, "they would never have let me tell the pupils that this Shah was rotten and that the religious chiefs of Tabriz were hardly any better" (p. 234).

Both teachers show us that teaching occurs in context and that pedagogy and technique is not the wellspring of moral choice. Teaching becomes the practice of freedom when it is guided by an unshakable commitment to working with human beings to reach the full measure of their humanity, and a willingness to reach toward a future fit for all.

In *A Lesson Before Dying*, Ernest Gaines (1993) creates a riveting portrait of a teacher locked in struggle with a resistant student, one wrestling with his own doubts and fears about himself as a teacher and a person, and straining against the outrages of the segregated South. Grant Wiggins has returned with considerable ambivalence to teach in the plantation school of his childhood. He feels trapped and longs to escape with his lover, another teacher named Vivian, to a place where he might breathe more freely, grow more fully, achieve something special. He had told his elderly Tante Lou, with whom he lives, "how much I hated this place and all I wanted to do was get away. I had told her I was no teacher, I hated teaching, and I was just running in place here. But she had not heard me . . ." (pp. 14–15).

The story begins in a courtroom with Tante Lou and her lifelong friend, Miss Emma, sitting stoic and still near the front. Emma's godson, Jefferson, was an unwitting participant in a failed liquor store stickup—his two companions and the store owner are dead—and as the sole survivor he is convicted of murder. The public defender, pleading for Jefferson's life, plays to the all-white jury with zeal:

> Gentlemen of the jury, look at this-this-this boy. I almost said man, but I can't say man. . . . I would call it a boy and a fool. A fool is not aware of right and wrong. . . .
>
> Do you see a man sitting here? . . . Look at the shape of the skull, this face as flat as the palm of my hand—look deeply into those eyes. Do you see a modicum of intelligence? . . . A cornered animal to strike quickly out of fear, a trait inherited from his ancestors in the deepest jungle of blackest Africa—yes, yes, that he can do—but to plan? . . . No, gentlemen, this skull here holds no plans. . . . A thing to hold the handle of a plow, a thing to load your bales of cotton . . . that is what you see here, but you do not see anything capable of planning a robbery or a murder. He does not even know the size of his clothes or his shoes. . . . Mention the names of Keats, Bryon, Scott, and see whether the eyes will show one moment of recognition. Ask him to describe a rose. . . . Gentlemen of the jury, this man planned

a robbery? Oh, pardon me, pardon me, I surely did not mean to insult your intelligence by saying "man" . . .

What justice would there be to take this life? Justice gentlemen? Why I would just as soon put a hog in the electric chair as this. (p. 78)

But this dehumanizing strategy doesn't work: Jefferson is sentenced to death. He has only a few weeks, perhaps a couple of months, to live. Devastating as the sentence is, it is that last plea from the public defender—that comparison of Jefferson to a hog—that cuts most deeply. "Called him a hog," says Miss Emma. And she turns to Grant Wiggins: "I don't want them to kill no hog" (p. 12). She wants Grant to visit Jefferson, to teach him to be a man before he dies.

Wiggins is deeply shaken by this:

What do I say to him? Do I know how a man is supposed to die? I'm still trying to find out how a man should live. Am I supposed to tell someone how to die who has never lived? . . .

Suppose . . . I reached him and made him realize that he was as much a man as any other man, then what? He's still going to die . . . so what will I have accomplished? What will I have done? Why not let the hog die without knowing anything? (p. 31)

Grant is haunted by the memory of his own former teacher, a bitter man: "You'll see that it'll take more than five and a half months to wipe away—peel—scrape away the blanket of ignorance that has been plastered and replastered over those brains in the past three hundred years. You'll see" (p. 64). The former mentor's message is that nothing a teacher in these circumstances does can matter or make a difference. Worse than that, Jefferson himself is wracked with hopelessness; he is uncooperative, and resistant: "It don't matter. . . . Nothing don't matter," (p. 73) he says, as he refuses to eat unless his food is put on the floor, like slops for a hog.

Grant begins by simply visiting Jefferson, being there, speaking sometimes, but mostly just sitting in silence. Witnessing. He brings Jefferson some small things: peanuts and pecans from his students, a small radio, a little notebook and a pencil. He encourages Jefferson to think of questions and write down his thoughts. And sometimes he accompanies Miss Emma, Tante Lou, and the reverend to the dayroom for visits. There he visits Jefferson and talks to him:

> I want to show them the difference between what they think you are and what you can be. To them, you're nothing but another nigger—no dignity, no heart, no love for your people. You can prove them wrong. You can do more than I can ever do. I have always done what they wanted me to do, teach reading, writing, and arithmetic. Nothing else—nothing about loving and caring. They never thought we were capable of learning those things. "Teach these niggers how to print their names and how to figure on their fingers." And I went along, but hating myself all the time for doing so . . .
>
> White people believe that they're better than anyone else on earth—and that's a myth. The last thing they want is to see a black man stand, and think, and show that common humanity that is in us all. It would destroy their myth . . .
>
> All we are, Jefferson, all of us on this earth, [is just] a piece of drifting wood, until we—each of us, individually—decide to be something else. I am still that piece of drifting wood . . . but you can be better. Because we need you to be and want you to be. . . . (pp. 191–193)

After Jefferson is electrocuted, a white deputy sheriff drives out to bring the news to Grant:

> "He was the strongest man in that crowded room, Grant Wiggins," Paul said, staring at me and speaking louder than was necessary. "He was, he was . . . he looked at the preacher and said, 'Tell Nannan I walked.' And straight he walked, Grant Wiggins. Straight he walked" . . .
>
> "You're one great teacher, Grant Wiggins," he said.

"I'm not great. I'm not even a teacher."

"Why do you say that?"

"You have to believe to be a teacher."

"I saw the transformation, Grant Wiggins," Paul said.

"I didn't do it."

"Who, then?"

"Maybe he did it himself."

"He never could have done that.

I saw the transformation. I'm a witness to that." (pp. 253–254)

A Lesson Before Dying is an essential teacher's tale, a story of growth and change for the teacher no less than the student, a story filled with mystery and improvisation, uncertainty, pain, and hope. While the circumstances are extreme, the interaction is recognizable. Teachers appreciate the irony of teaching what we ourselves neither fully know nor understand. Each of us can remember other teachers who counseled us not to teach, and each of us recognizes the resistant student, the student who refuses to learn. We can each uncover moments of intense self-reflection, consciousness shifts, and personal growth spurred by our students and our attempts to teach.

Many teachers also know what it means to teach against the grain. Against oppression, opposition, and obstinacy. Against a history of evil. Against glib assumptions. When the sheriff compares education to agitation and the teacher to an organizer "trying to put something in his head against his will," one is reminded of Frederick Douglass's master exploding in anger when he discovers that his wife has taught the young Douglass to read: "It will unfit him to be a slave." One is reminded as well of the charge "outside agitator," hurled by the bosses at the union organizer, or by the college trustees at student radicals. When the sheriff grins at Wiggins for giving Jefferson a journal, because a hog can't write authentic thoughts or experience real human feelings, we are in a familiar space. And when Jefferson writes in the journal, "I cry cause you been so good to me Mr. Wiggin and nobody ain't never been that good to me an make me think I'm somebody" (Gaines, 1993, p. 232), we recognize the ethical dimension and the soul of teaching.

We can't really speak of freedom and schools in America without remembering the great Civil Rights Movement that emerged in the middle of the last century. A central goal of the Movement had been access to excellent education, and schools became an open site of struggle and energy and hope from 1954 until today. But vehicles for all the Movement's activities—voter registration, tactical training, research—were Freedom Schools and Citizenship Schools, created by activists for specific purposes and campaigns. Together they were the venue for public participation, the places where people found their voices, their courage, their power.

There's a story we tell ourselves today about race and racism, about the Civil Rights Movement: that everybody knows, or so it seems, that it was a good thing. It's an account told and retold until it's become central to our national identity and psyche. The story is about a long-ago time when racial segregation was legal and some racist white people mistreated black people in this country. There arose then a leader, a preacher who became the Moses of his people, leading them out of bondage and into a promised land. Martin Luther King Jr. is a national hero, it's said, because his vision and courage convinced everyone to oppose racism, and sparked a movement that changed the face of the nation.

It's a nice story, a satisfying and reassuring story, but it's also in large measure a story fashioned in the hazy glow of memory.

In reality the Movement was messy, idiosyncratic, and improvisational, filled with conflict and contradiction, and failure upon failure. Its goal was never national legislation nor simply "civil rights." There was a large hope for wider social change, for economic and social justice, for dignity and an end to terror. The Movement was always painfully aware, even in its most glorious moments, of how much further there was to go.

If the mythical, iconic story were true, how could we explain that our schools and our cities are more segregated today than they were 50 years ago, that black children are more than twice as likely to fail as their white counterparts, or that a million black men are caught up in our criminal justice system? How can we understand that disenfranchisement laws (permanently denying the vote to people convicted of a felony, even those who now work and pay taxes) are concentrated in the South and deny 5 million Americans, disproportionately black Americans, the right to vote, and bar a quarter of black men from voting in Mississippi, Alabama, and, most telling since the 2000 election, Florida? If this is racism disappeared, how is it that statistics say a white male born in 1998 will live 74.5 years compared to 67.6 years for a black male, or that a black man is more than twice as likely to be murdered as a white man, or that the median net worth of a black family in 1993 was $4,418 compared to $45,740 for a white family? How to understand that Chicago schools, over 80% black and 15% recent immigrants, are asked to survive on less resources than surrounding districts, even though they serve half the poorest students and three-quarters of the bilingual children in Illinois? Everything is not, then, settled. Now as then, everything is in contention.

The people who fought Martin Luther King Jr. tooth and claw in life are the same ones who fervently promote the fairy-tale King now that he's safely in the ground. They, too, have a dream, a dream that no one will notice that they continue to profit and benefit from the subtle structures of oppression built on race.

The Martin Luther King icon, the King of the "I Have a Dream" speech and the Nobel Peace Prize and benevolent social progress, is a gross reduction of the living, breathing King, the man who denounced war and militarism, fought for economic justice, and angrily demanded deeper structural changes in society. That King, too, is worth remembering.

Rosa Parks is similarly remembered for an act of courage, her refusal to move to the back of the bus in Montgomery,

Alabama, on December 1, 1955. This act initiated the dramatic yearlong bus boycott that catapulted Martin Luther King Jr. to leadership and national prominence. Rosa Parks's courage, dignity, and determination are rightly celebrated.

What is perhaps less known is that during the previous summer, Rosa Parks had participated in a leadership workshop led by Septima Clark at the Highlander Folk School. Parks had been the leader of the NAACP youth group in Montgomery and was well known as a local activist. She had organized a group of young black people to attend a traveling exhibit from Washington, D.C.—the "Freedom Train"—that carried the original Constitution and Declaration of Independence. Whites didn't want to enter the exhibit side by side with blacks, but the exhibit was integrated, and Rosa Parks made a point of exercising her right and the rights of the black children to go through the exhibit as equals. Afterward she became a target of abuse and harassment.

Rosa Parks attended the Highlander workshop and told her story. The workshops typically began by asking people what they needed to know, and they always ended with the question: "What are you going to do back home?" Parks noted that Montgomery was the "cradle of the Confederacy" (Clark, 1986, p. 33) and that little was possible because of how difficult conditions were and how hard it was for the black people there to stick together. But she said she would continue her work with the young people, that they were the hope for the future, and that she would continue to teach them about their rights. She was given encouragement and pledges of support. Three months later she was arrested. When Septima Clark heard the news, she said, "Rosa? Rosa? She was so shy when she came to Highlander, but she got enough courage to do that" (p. 34).

Septima Clark was a founder of the Citizenship Schools, and education director at Highlander for many years. When she taught reading she "put down 'de' for 'the,' because that's the way they said 'the.'" She told her students that in books they would see the word "the": "You say 'de,' but in the book it's printed 'the'" (p. 106).

She taught beginning reading by creating homemade books based on the experiences of the people who attended the schools:

> I wrote their stories on the dry cleaner's bags, stories of their country right around them, where they walked to come to school, the things that grew around them, what they could see in the skies. They told them to me, and I wrote them on dry cleaner's bags and tacked them on the wall. (p. 106)

Later, after students could read stories of their own island, she brought in books and stories that could open them to a world beyond their experiences. These "vicarious experiences" told of "great corn fields in the midwest where farmers made thousands of dollars," (p. 107) and of seals and mountains and cities. As a teacher, Septima Clark built on a foundation of what students knew and challenged them to move from the known to the unknown. She strengthened her students in two directions: affirming their humanity and their life experiences, serving as a cultural and personal mirror for them, she exposed obstacles to their freedom; she also opened a wider world to them, introducing them to the unknown and unexperienced through the various literacies that connected them to other people and other times.

The Citizenship Schools applied this fundamental lesson about teaching to the huge task of educating a whole community. As she recruited people to teach in the Citizenship Schools, Clark began with an understanding of the students, of how they experienced the world:

> We had a day-by-day plan, which started the first night with them talking, telling us what they would like to learn. The next morning we started off with asking them: "Do you have an employment office in your town? Where is it located? What hours is it open? Have you been there to get work?" (p. 63)

The answers to those things we wrote down on dry cleaner's bags, so they could read them . . .

We were trying to make teachers out of people who could barely read and write. But they could teach. If they could read at all, we could teach them that c-o-n-s-t-i-t-u-t-i-o-n spells constitution. We'd have a long discussion all morning about what the constitution was. . . . (pp. 63–64)

The power of the lesson was both form and content. People left the teacher education sessions to lead their own projects of voter registration and community education: they discussed the problems and the needs of people in their own local communities; they posed questions ("How come the pavement stops where the black section begins?"); and they organized a process that allowed for discovery and connection. The teachers listened and "let them know that we felt they were right according to the kind of thing that they had in their mind, but according to living in this world there were other things they needed to know." The starting points for teaching were various and complex (how the local government functions, how the sharecropping system works, how to keep a bank account and avoid being cheated), but the goals were the same: affirmation, growth, and power.

This kind of education opposes fear, ignorance, and helplessness by strengthening knowledge and ability. It enables people to question, to wonder, and to look critically. It requires teachers who are thoughtful, caring, and connected deeply to those they teach. This enabling education can be both the process by which people discover and develop various capacities as they locate themselves historically, and the vehicle for moving forward and breaking through the immutable facts, traditions, and objects of life as we find them. Its singular value is that it is education for freedom.

Learning to read in the old South was a subversive activity, an activity that many thought could change the fundamental structure of the Jim Crow system. Many in the South considered black illiteracy a pillar of white supremacy. The Citizenship Schools, which paralleled the heroic efforts to educate ex-slaves during the radical period of Black Reconstruction immediately following the Civil War, challenged white supremacy by teaching basic literacy, encouraging people to vote, and providing alternatives and a sense of efficacy. The first Citizenship School organized at Johns Island was disguised as a grocery store "to fool white people." Reading represented power; for black people it was the power to control and to change their destiny.

Education for freedom is always more a possibility than an accomplishment, more an achievement of people in action than a finished condition. It requires a continual identification of what is to be done, a constant process of unfolding and moving forward. The process of education, of discovery, of freedom, is never neat, logical, smooth, or obvious in advance. It is more often messy, rough, unpredictable, and inconsistent. It can be halting and it can be slow, but it can also surprise with the suddenness and power of change.

The sense of freedom embodied in the Citizenship and Freedom Schools is linked to action, to a sense of solidarity and community. It is different from the sense of freedom as interior or individual. And yet there are some common edges, and perhaps teachers today can imagine and strive for a new synthesis. Neill's emphasis on the individual does not require a rejection of community; Clark's focus on the group does not obliterate the dignity and value and sacredness of the individual. A contemporary challenge is to bring these two visions of freedom to life in today's classrooms.

Education lives an excruciating paradox precisely because of its association with and location in schools. Education is about opening doors, opening minds, opening possibilities. School is too often on a mission of sorting and punishing, grading and ranking and certifying. Education is unconditional, asking nothing in return. School usually demands obedience and conformity as a precondition to attendance. Education is surprising and unruly and disorderly and free, while the first and fundamental law of school is to follow orders. Education frees the mind, the spirit, the actor in each of us, while schooling bureaucratizes the brain. An educator unleashes the unpredictable, while too many schoolteachers start with an unhealthy obsession with classroom management and linear lesson plans.

Working in schools—where the fundamental truths and demands and possibilities of teaching at its best are obscured and diminished and opaque, and where the powerful ethical core of our efforts is systematically defaced and erased— requires a reengagement with the larger purposes of teaching. When the drumbeat of our daily lives is all about controlling the crowd, managing and moving the mob, conveying disembodied bits of information to inert things propped at desks before us, the need to fight for ourselves and our students becomes an imperative. Central to that fight is the understanding that there is no basis for education in a democracy except for a faith in freedom and the enduring capacity for growth in ordinary people, in individuals, and in community.

Teaching for freedom goes beyond presenting what already is; it is teaching toward what ought to be. It is more than structures and guidelines; it includes an exposure to and understanding of material realities—advantages and disadvantages, privileges and oppressions—as well. Teaching of this kind might stir people to come together as vivid, thoughtful and, yes, outraged. Students might find themselves dissatisfied with what had only yesterday seemed to be the natural order of things. At this point, when consciousness links to conduct and upheaval is in the air, teaching becomes a call to freedom.

The fundamental message of the teacher begins with this: You can change your life. Whoever you are, wherever you've been, whatever you've done, the teacher invites you to see the world anew. The teacher posits possibility, openness, and alternative; the teacher points to what could be, but is not yet. The teacher's basic rule is to reach.

To teach consciously for ethical action adds a complicating element to that fundamental message, making it more layered, more dense, more excruciatingly difficult to enact, and simultaneously sturdier, more engaging, more powerful, and much of the time more joyful. Teaching for ethical action demands a dialectical stance. One eye is firmly fixed on the students. Who are they? What are their hopes and dreams? Their passions and commitments? What skills, abilities, and capacities does each one bring to the classroom? The other eye is looking unblinkingly at the concentric circles of context—historical flow, cultural surround, economic reality. Teaching as the practice of freedom is teaching that arouses students, engages them in a quest to identify obstacles to their full humanity and the life chances of others, and then to drive, to move against those obstacles. At this level the fundamental message of the teacher becomes: You must change the world.

ELEVEN

On the Side of the Child

Neill taught through anecdote, a non-authoritative style that announces his democratic intentions. His pronouncements are sometimes authoritative, but in other ways Neill was the anti-guru, the non-Oz.

Each of the four hopeful seekers skipping together down the yellow brick road toward Oz, singing their desires to one another and to the heavens, has diagnosed a deficiency, identified a lack, recognized a need. Each has become painfully conscious of something missing, a hole in need of repair. Each is stirred to action against an obstacle to his or her fullness, and each gathers momentum and power from the others, from intimate relationships forged through collective struggle. They know what's wrong and they're off to see a wizard who will make everything right.

This is not a bad start for teachers seeking a vocabulary of basic qualities in their quest for wholeness and for goodness in teaching—a home, a heart, a brain, the nerve. There is more, to be sure, but these are essential if we want to teach for freedom, following our own yellow brick roads into the beyond.

Teaching is intellectual and ethical work; it takes a thoughtful, reflective, and caring person to do it well. It takes a brain and a heart. The first and fundamental challenge for teachers is to embrace students as three-dimensional creatures, as distinct human beings with hearts and minds and skills and dreams and capacities of their own, as people much like ourselves. This embrace is initially an act of faith—we must assume capacity even when it is not immediately available or visible—because we work most often in places where aggregating and grouping kids on the flimsiest evidence is the reigning practice, where the suffocating habit of labeling youngsters on the basis of their deficits is commonplace. A teacher needs a brain to break through the cotton wool smothering the mind, to see beyond the blizzard of labels to this specific child, trembling and whole and real, and to this one, and to the next. And a teacher needs a heart to fully grasp the importance of that gesture, to recognize in the deepest core of one's being that every child is precious, each an original, the one and only who will ever trod this earth, deserving enlightenment, freedom, and the best a teacher can give—respect, awe, reverence, and commitment.

A teacher who takes up this challenge is a teacher working against the grain—you've got to have the nerve. All the pressures that push teachers to act as clerks and functionaries—interchangeable parts in a vast, gleaming, and highly rationalized production line—must somehow be resisted. To teach with a heart and a brain—to see education as a deeply humanizing enterprise, to teach toward freedom and the opening of infinite possibilities for your students—requires courage. Courage is a quality nurtured in solidarity with others; it is an achievement of colleagues. In order to teach with thought and care and courage, you really need a home.

The four seekers lurching toward Oz provide another lesson for us: they teach us we can all constantly work to identify obstacles to our freedom and our fullness. The obstacles will change as we develop and grow, but there is always more to know, always more to become, always something to overcome. In our quest we can all reach out for allies and friends to give us strength and heart and the courage to move on. And we can know at the start that there is no wizard at the end of the road, that every guru is part fraud, that there is no higher power with a magic wand to solve our all-too-human problems.

Neill knew that his own mentors, Reich and Lane, were flawed, that "every idol has feet of clay" (1992, p. 214), and he was somewhat embarrassed at having once been a disciple, and later in life a bit horrified at what lay in store for him: "I'd hate to think that long after I am dead teachers will call themselves

Summerhillians. They will thus advertise the fact that they are dead" (1992, p. 70).

His motto had become "Take from each what you want and reject the rest, and never label yourself as one of a school" (1992, p. 70). In the spirit of freedom, Neill is urging each of us to take full responsibility with what we know, what we guess, what we believe and feel, what we do. We can't fall back to justify ourselves by claiming a neat but ultimately false label: "I'm a Christian," "I'm a Marxist," "I'm a professor." Beyond this, Neill echoes Dewey: "My enemies are bad enough, but my friends are so much worse." Jay Featherstone once defined a conservative as someone who worships a dead radical. Whatever we do, let's not lionize Neill.

We must recognize that the people with the problems are also the people with the solutions, and that waiting for the lawmakers, the system, the union, or a wizard to get it right before we get it right is to wait a lifetime. We can look inside ourselves, summon strengths we never knew we had, connect up with teachers and parents and kids to create the schools and classrooms we deserve—thoughtful places of decency, oases of peace and freedom and justice. We are on the way, then, to our real emerald cities.

The spirit of Summerhill is a wild and unruly quest for freedom. Life is a restless voyage, and we are its sailors. The function of education is to create us as more fully human—more powerful, engaged, connected, thoughtful, and caring—more capable of taking the oars and the helm of our own ships. Students, then, are constructors of their own lives, narrators of their own histories, citizens of their own schools, rather than casual visitors or accidental tourists in *our* spaces. For teachers the humanizing work begins in nourishing, supporting, and challenging our students. Born in faith and reverence, punctuated by surprise, amazement, shock, forgiveness, awe, humility, our work is all about relationships. We would do well to hold up the banner of *freedom*, and with Neill join the believers in life against the forces of death, on the side of the child.

References

Arendt, H. (1954). *Between past and future: Eight exercises in political thought.* New York: Penguin.

Arendt, H. (1963). *On revolution.* New York: Penguin.

Baldwin, J. (1996). A talk to teachers. In W. Ayers & P. Ford (Eds.), *City Kids/City Teachers* (pp. 219–227). New York: The New Press.

Brooks, G. (1983). Boy breaking glass. In A. W. Allison et al. (Eds.), *Norton anthology of poetry* (3rd ed.). New York: W. W. Norton and Company.

DuBois, W.E.B. (2002). *Dubois on education.* E. F. Provenzo, (Ed.). Walnut Creek, CA: AltaMira Press.

Carger, C. (1996) *Of borders and dreams.* New York: Teachers College Press.

Clark, S. (1986). *Ready from within.* Novarro, CA: Wild Tree Press.

Gaines, E. (1993) *A lesson before dying.* New York: Knopf.

Ginzberg, N. (1989). *The little virtues* (D. Davis, Trans.). New York: Arcade Publishing.

Horton, M., with Kohl, H., & Kohl, J. (1990). *The long haul.* New York: Doubleday.

Kozol, J. (1992). *Savage inequalities.* New York: Harper Perennial.

Lessing, D. (1972). *The golden notebook.* London: Pantheon Books. (Originally published 1962)

Lessing, D. (1994). *Under my skin.* New York: HarperCollins.

Maalouf, A. (1994). *Samarkand* (R. Harris, trans.). London: Abacus.

Neill, A. S. (1960). *Summerhill: A radical approach to child rearing.* New York, Hart Publishing.

Neill, A. S. (1992). *Summerhill school: A new view of childhood.* A. Lamb (Ed.). New York: St. Martin's Griffin.

Oe, K. (1995). *Nip the buds, shoot the kids.* New York: Grove Press.

Rose, M. (1995). *Possible lives: The promise of public education in America.* New York: Penguin Books.

Stein, A. (1971, May). Strategies for failure. *Harvard Educational Review, 41*(2), 158–204.

White, E. B. (1945). *Stuart Little.* New York: Harper & Row.

SELECTIONS FROM

Summerhill:
A Radical Approach to Child Rearing

A. S. NEILL

A Word of Introduction

In psychology, no man knows very much. The inner forces of human life are still largely hidden from us.

Since Freud's genius made it alive, psychology has gone far; but it is still a new science, mapping out the coast of an unknown continent. Fifty years hence, psychologists will very likely smile at our ignorance of today.

Since I left education and took up child psychology, I have had all sorts of children to deal with—incendiaries, thieves, liars, bed-wetters, and bad-tempered children. Years of intensive work in child training has convinced me that I know comparatively little of the forces that motivate life. I am convinced, however, that parents who have had to deal with only their own children know much less than I do.

It is because I believe that a difficult child is nearly always made difficult by wrong treatment at home that I dare address parents.

What is the province of psychology? I suggest the word *curing*. But what kind of curing? I do not want to be cured of my habit of choosing the colors orange and black; nor do I want to be cured of smoking; nor of my liking for a bottle of beer. No teacher has the right to cure a child of making noises on a drum. The only curing that should be practiced is the curing of unhappiness.

The difficult child is the child who is unhappy. He is at war with himself; and in consequence, he is at war with the world.

The difficult adult is in the same boat. No happy man ever disturbed a meeting, or preached a war, or lynched a Negro. No happy woman ever nagged her husband or her children. No happy man ever committed a murder or a theft. No happy employer ever frightened his employees.

All crimes, all hatreds, all wars can be reduced to unhappiness. This book is an attempt to show how unhappiness arises, how it ruins human lives, and how children can be reared so that much of this unhappiness will never arise.

More than that, this book is the story of a place—Summerhill—where children's unhappiness is cured and, more important, where children are reared in happiness.

The Idea of Summerhill

This is a story of a modern school—Summerhill.

Summerhill was founded in the year 1921. The school is situated within the village of Leiston, in Suffolk, England, and is about one hundred miles from London.

Just a word about Summerhill pupils. Some children come to Summerhill at the age of five years, and others as late as fifteen. The children generally remain at the school until they are sixteen years old. We generally have about twenty-five boys and twenty girls.

The children are divided into three age groups: The youngest range from five to seven, the intermediates from eight to ten, and the oldest from eleven to fifteen.

Generally we have a fairly large sprinkling of children from foreign countries. At the present time (1960) we have five Scandinavians, one Hollander, one German and one American.

The children are housed by age groups with a house mother for each group. The intermediates sleep in a stone building, the seniors sleep in huts. Only one or two older pupils have rooms for themselves. The boys live two or three or four to a room, and so do the girls. The pupils do not have to stand room inspection and no one picks up after them. They are left free. No one tells them what to wear: they put on any kind of costume they want to at any time.

Newspapers call it a *Go-as-you-please School* and imply that it is a gathering of wild primitives who know no law and have no manners.

It seems necessary, therefore, for me to write the story of Summerhill as honestly as I can. That I write with a bias is natural; yet I shall try to show the demerits of Summerhill as well as its merits. Its merits will be the merits of healthy, free children whose lives are unspoiled by fear and hate.

Obviously, a school that makes active children sit at desks studying mostly useless subjects is a bad school. It is a good school only for those who believe in *such* a school, for those uncreative citizens who want docile, uncreative children who will fit into a civilization whose standard of success is money.

Summerhill began as an experimental school. It is no longer such; it is now a demonstration school, for it demonstrates that freedom works.

When my first wife and I began the school, we had one main idea: *to make the school fit the child*—instead of making the child fit the school.

I had taught in ordinary schools for many years. I knew the other way well. I knew it was all wrong. It was wrong because it was based on an adult conception of what a child should be and of how a child should learn. The other way dated from the days when psychology was still an unknown science.

Well, we set out to make a school in which we should allow children freedom to be themselves. In order to do this, we had to renounce all discipline, all direction, all suggestion, all moral training, all religious instruction. We have been called brave, but it did not require courage. All it required was what we had—a complete belief in the child as a good, not an evil, being. For almost forty years, this belief in the goodness of the child has never wavered; it rather has become a final faith.

My view is that a child is innately wise and realistic. If left to himself without adult suggestion of any kind, he will develop as far as he is capable of developing. Logically, Summerhill is a place in which people who have the innate ability and wish to be scholars will be scholars; while those who are only fit to sweep the streets will sweep the streets. But we have not produced a street cleaner so far. Nor do I write this snobbishly, for I would rather see a school produce a happy street cleaner than a neurotic scholar.

What is Summerhill like? Well, for one thing, lessons are optional. Children can go to them or stay away from them—for years if they want to. There *is* a timetable—but only for the teachers.

The children have classes usually according to their age, but sometimes according to their interests. We have no new methods of teaching, because we do not consider that teaching in itself matters very much. Whether a school has or has not a special method for teaching long division is of no significance, for long division is of no importance except to those who *want* to learn it. And the child who *wants* to learn long division *will* learn it no matter how it is taught.

Children who come to Summerhill as kindergarteners attend lessons from the beginning of their stay; but pupils from other schools vow that they will never attend any beastly lessons again at any time. They play and cycle and get in people's way, but they fight shy of lessons. This sometimes goes on for months. The recovery time is proportionate to the hatred their last school gave them. Our record case was a girl from a convent. She loafed for three years. The average period of recovery from lesson aversion is three months.

Strangers to this idea of freedom will be wondering what sort of madhouse it is where children play all day if they want to. Many an adult says, "If I had been sent to a school like that, I'd never have done a thing." Others say, "Such children will feel themselves heavily handicapped when they have to compete against children who have been made to learn."

I think of Jack who left us at the age of seventeen to go into an engineering factory. One day, the managing director sent for him.

"You are the lad from Summerhill," he said. "I'm curious to know how such an education appears to you now that you are mixing with lads from the old schools. Suppose you had to choose again, would you go to Eton or Summerhill?"

"Oh, Summerhill, of course," replied Jack.

"But what does it offer that the other schools don't offer?"

Jack scratched his head. "I dunno," he said slowly; "I think it gives you a feeling of complete self-confidence."

"Yes," said the manager dryly, "I noticed it when you came into the room."

"Lord," laughed Jack, "I'm sorry if I gave you that impression."

"I liked it," said the director. "Most men when I call them into the office fidget about and look uncomfortable. You came in as my equal. By the way, what department did you say you would like to transfer to?"

This story shows that learning in itself is not as important as personality and character. Jack failed in his university exams because he hated book learning. But his lack of knowledge about *Lamb's Essays* or the French language did not handicap him in life. He is now a successful engineer.

All the same, there is a lot of learning in Summerhill. Perhaps a group of our twelve-year-olds could not compete with a class of equal age in handwriting or spelling or fractions. But in an examination requiring originality, our lot would beat the others hollow.

We have no class examinations in the school, but sometimes I set an exam for fun. The following questions appeared in one such paper:

Where are the following:—Madrid, Thursday Island, yesterday, love, democracy, hate, my pocket screwdriver (alas, there was no helpful answer to that one).

Give meanings for the following: (the number shows how many are expected for each)—Hand (3) . . . only two got the third right—the standard of measure for a horse. Brass (4) . . . metal, cheek, top army officers, department of an orchestra. Translate Hamlet's To-be-or-not-to-be speech into Summerhillese.

These questions are obviously not intended to be serious, and the children enjoy them thoroughly. Newcomers, on the whole, do not rise to the answering standard of pupils who have become acclimatized to the school. Not that they have less brain power, but rather because they have become so accustomed to work in a serious groove that any light touch puzzles them.

This is the play side of our teaching. In all classes much work is done. If, for some reason, a teacher cannot take his class on the appointed day, there is usually much disappointment for the pupils.

David, aged nine, had to be isolated for whooping cough. He cried bitterly. "I'll miss Roger's lesson in geography," he protested. David had been in the school practically from birth, and he had definite and final ideas about the necessity of having his lessons given to him. David is now a lecturer in mathematics at London University.

A few years ago someone at a General School Meeting (at which all school rules are voted by the entire school, each pupil and each staff member having one vote) proposed that a certain culprit should be punished by being banished from lessons for a week. The other children protested on the ground that the punishment was too severe.

My staff and I have a hearty hatred of all examinations. To us, the university exams are anathema. But we cannot refuse to teach children the required subjects. Obviously, as long as the exams are in existence, they are our master. Hence, the Summerhill staff is always qualified to teach to the set standard.

Not that many children want to take these exams; only those going to the university do so. And such children do not seem to find it especially hard to tackle these exams. They generally begin to work for them seriously at the age of fourteen, and they do the work in about three years. Of course they don't always pass at the first try. The more important fact is that they try again.

Summerhill is possibly the happiest school in the world. We have no truants and seldom a case of homesickness. We very rarely have fights—quarrels, of course, but seldom have I seen a stand-up fight like the ones we used to have as boys. I seldom hear a child cry, because children when free have much less hate to express than children who are downtrodden. Hate breeds hate, and love breeds love. Love means approving of children, and that is essential in any school. You can't be on the side of children if you punish them and storm at them. Summerhill is a school in which the child knows that he is approved of.

Mind you, we are not above and beyond human foibles. I spent weeks planting potatoes one spring, and when I found eight plants pulled up in June, I made a big fuss. Yet there was a difference between my fuss and that of an authoritarian. My fuss was about potatoes, but the fuss an authoritarian would have made would have dragged in the question of morality— right and wrong. I did not say that it was wrong to steal my spuds; I did not make it a matter of good and evil—I made it a matter of *my spuds*. They were *my* spuds and they should have been left alone. I hope I am making the distinction clear.

Let me put it another way. To the children, I am no authority to be feared. I am their equal, and the row I kick up about my spuds has no more significance to them than the row a boy may kick up about his punctured bicycle tire. It is quite safe to have a row with a child when you are equals.

Now some will say: "That's all bunk. There can't be equality. Neill is the boss; he is bigger and wiser." That is indeed true. I am the boss, and if the house caught fire the children would run to me. They know that I am bigger and more knowledgeable, but that does not matter when I meet them on their own ground, the potato patch, so to speak.

When Billy, aged five, told me to get out of his birthday party because I hadn't been invited, I went at once without hesitation—just as Billy gets out of my room when I don't want his company. It is not easy to describe this relationship between teacher and child, but every visitor to Summerhill knows what I mean when I say that the relationship is ideal. One sees it in the attitude to the staff in general. Rudd, the chemistry man, is Derek. Other members of the staff are known as Harry, and Ulla, and Pam. I am Neill, and the cook is Esther.

In Summerhill, everyone has equal rights. No one is allowed to walk on my grand piano, and I am not allowed to borrow a boy's cycle without his permission. At a General School Meeting, the vote of a child of six counts for as much as my vote does.

But, says the knowing one, in practice of course the voices of the grownups count. Doesn't the child of six wait to see how you vote before he raises his hand? I wish he sometimes would, for too many of my proposals are beaten. Free children are not easily influenced; the absence of fear accounts for this phenomenon. Indeed, the absence of fear is the finest thing that can happen to a child.

Our children do not fear our staff. One of the school rules is that after ten o'clock at night there shall be quietness on the upper corridor. One night, about eleven, a pillow fight was going on, and I left my desk, where I was writing, to protest against the row. As I got upstairs, there was a scurrying of feet and the corridor was empty and quiet. Suddenly I heard a disappointed voice say, "Humph, it's only Neill," and the fun began again at once. When I explained that I was trying to write a book downstairs, they showed concern and at once agreed to chuck the noise. Their scurrying came from the suspicion that their bedtime officer (one of their own age) was on their track.

I emphasize the importance of this absence of fear of adults. A child of nine will come and tell me he has broken a window with a ball. He tells me, because he isn't afraid of arousing wrath or moral indignation. He may have to pay for the window, but he doesn't have to fear being lectured or being punished.

There was a time some years back when the School Government resigned, and no one would stand for election. I seized the opportunity of putting up a notice: "In the absence of a government, I herewith declare myself Dictator. Heil Neill!" Soon there were mutterings. In the afternoon Vivien, aged six, came to me and said, "Neill, I've broken a window in the gym."

I waved him away. "Don't bother me with little things like that," I said, and he went.

A little later he came back and said he had broken two windows. By this time I was curious, and asked him what the great idea was.

"I don't like dictators," he said, "and I don't like going without my grub." (I discovered later that the opposition to dictatorship had tried to take itself out on the cook, who promptly shut up the kitchen and went home.)

"Well," I asked, "what are you going to do about it?"

"Break more windows," he said doggedly.

"Carry on," I said, and he carried on.

When he returned, he announced that he had broken seventeen windows. "But mind," he said earnestly, "I'm going to pay for them."

"How?"

"Out of my pocket money. How long will it take me?"

I did a rapid calculation. "About ten years," I said.

He looked glum for a minute; then I saw his face light up.

"Gee," he cried, "I don't have to pay for them at all."

"But what about the private property rule?" I asked. "The windows are my private property."

"I know that but there isn't any private property rule now. There isn't any government, and the government makes the rules."

It may have been my expression that made him add, "But all the same I'll pay for them."

But he didn't have to pay for them. Lecturing in London shortly afterward, I told the story; and at the end of my talk, a young man came up and handed me a pound note "to pay for the young devil's windows." Two years later, Vivien was still telling people of his windows and of the man who paid for them. "He must have been a terrible fool, because he never even saw me.

Children make contact with strangers more easily when fear is unknown to them. English reserve is, at bottom, really fear; and that is why the most reserved are those who have the most wealth. The fact that Summerhill children are so exceptionally friendly to visitors and strangers is a source of pride to me and my staff.

We must confess, however, that many of our visitors are people of interest to the children. The kind of visitor most unwelcome to them is the teacher, especially the earnest teacher, who wants to see their drawing and written work. The most welcome visitor is the one who has good tales to tell—of adventure and travel or, best of all, of aviation. A boxer or a good tennis player is surrounded at once, but visitors who spout theory are left severely alone.

The most frequent remark that visitors make is that they cannot tell who is staff and who is pupil. It is true: the feeling of unity is that strong when children are approved of. There is no deference to a teacher as a teacher. Staff and pupils have the same food and have to obey the same community laws. The children would resent any special privileges given to the staff.

When I used to give the staff a talk on psychology every week, there was a muttering that it wasn't fair. I changed the plan and made the talks open to everyone over twelve. Every Tuesday night, my room is filled with eager youngsters who not only listen but give their opinions freely. Among the subjects the children have asked me to talk about have been these: The Inferiority Complex, The Psychology of Stealing, The Psychology of the Gangster, The Psychology of Humor, Why Did Man Become a Moralist?, Masturbation, Crowd Psychology. It is obvious that such children will go out into life with a broad clear knowledge of themselves and others.

The most frequent question asked by Summerhill visitors is, "Won't the child turn round and blame the school for not making him learn arithmetic or music?" The answer is that young Freddy Beethoven and young Tommy Einstein will refuse to be kept away from their respective spheres.

The function of the child is to live his own life—not the life that his anxious parents think he should live, nor a life according to the purpose of the educator who thinks he knows what is best. All this interference and guidance on the part of adults only produces a generation of robots.

You cannot *make* children learn music or anything else without to some degree converting them into will-less adults. You fashion them into accepters of the *status quo*—a good thing for a society that needs obedient sitters at dreary desks, standers in shops, mechanical catchers of the 8:30 suburban train—a society, in short, that is carried on the shabby shoulders of the scared little man—the scared-to-death conformist.

Summerhill Education vs. Standard Education

I hold that the aim of life is to find happiness, which means to find interest. Education should be a preparation for life. Our culture has not been very successful. Our education, politics, and economics lead to war. Our medicines have not done away with disease. Our religion has not abolished usury and robbery. Our boasted humanitarianism still allows public opinion to approve of the barbaric sport of hunting. The advances of the age are advances in mechanism—in radio and television, in electronics, in jet planes. New world wars threaten, for the world's social conscience is still primitive.

If we feel like questioning today, we can pose a few awkward questions. Why does man seem to have many more diseases than animals have? Why does man hate and kill in war when animals do not? Why does cancer increase? Why are there so many suicides? So many insane sex crimes? Why the hate that is anti-Semitism? Why Negro hating and lynching? Why backbiting and spite? Why is sex obscene and a leering joke? Why is being a bastard a social disgrace? Why the continuance of religions that have long ago lost their love and hope and charity? Why, a thousand whys about our vaunted state of civilized eminence!

I ask these questions because I am by profession a teacher, one who deals with the young. I ask these questions because those so often asked by teachers are the unimportant ones, the ones about school subjects. I ask what earthly good can come out of discussions about French or ancient history or what not when these subjects don't matter a jot compared to the larger question of life's natural fulfillment—of man's inner happiness.

How much of our education is real doing, real self-expression? Handwork is too often the making of a pin tray under the eye of an expert. Even the Montessori system, well-known as a system of directed play, is an artificial way of making the child learn by doing. It has nothing creative about it.

In the home, the child is always being taught. In almost every home, there is always at least one ungrown-up grownup who rushes to show Tommy how his new engine works. There is always someone to lift the baby up on a chair when baby wants to examine something on the wall. Every time we show Tommy how his engine works we are stealing from that child the joy of life—the joy of discovery—the joy of overcoming an obstacle. Worse! We make that child come to believe that he is inferior, and must depend on help.

Parents are slow in realizing how unimportant the learning side of school is. Children, like adults, learn what they want to learn. All prize-giving and marks and exams sidetrack proper personality development. Only pedants claim that learning from books is education.

Books are the least important apparatus in a school. All that any child needs is the three R's; the rest should be tools and clay and sports and theater and paint and freedom.

Most of the school work that adolescents do is simply a waste of time, of energy, of patience. It robs youth of its right to play and play and play; it puts old heads on young shoulders.

When I lecture to students at teacher training colleges and universities, I am often shocked at the ungrownupness of these lads and lasses stuffed with useless knowledge. They know a lot; they shine in dialectics; they can quote the classics—but in their outlook on life many of them are infants. For they have been taught *to know*, but have not been allowed *to feel*. These students are friendly, pleasant, eager, but something is lacking—emotional factor, the power to subordinate thinking to feeling. I talk to these of a world they have missed and go on missing. Their textbooks do not deal with human character, or with love, or with freedom, or with self-determination. And so the system goes on, aiming only at standards of book learning—goes on separating the head from the heart.

It is time that we were challenging the school's notion of work. It is taken for granted that every child should learn mathematics, history, geography, some science, a little art, and certainly literature. It is time we realized that the average young child is not much interested in any of these subjects.

I prove this with every new pupil. When told that the school is free, every new pupil cries, "Hurrah! You won't catch me doing dull arithmetic and things!"

I am not decrying learning. But, learning should come after play. And learning should not be deliberately seasoned with play to make it palatable.

Learning is important—but not to everyone. Nijinsky could not pass his school exams in St. Petersburg, and he could not enter the State Ballet without passing those exams. He simply could not learn school subjects—his mind was elsewhere. They faked an exam for him, giving him the answers with the papers—so a biography says. What a loss to the world if Nijinsky had had to really pass those exams!

Creators learn what they want to learn in order to have the tools that their originality and genius demand. We do not know how much creation is killed in the classroom with its emphasis on learning.

I have seen a girl weep nightly over her geometry. Her mother wanted her to go to the university, but the girl's whole soul was artistic. I was delighted when I heard that she had failed her college entrance exams for the seventh time. Possibly, the mother would now allow her to go on the stage as she longed to do.

Some time ago, I met a girl of fourteen in Copenhagen who had spent three years in Summerhill and had spoken perfect English here. "I suppose you are at the top of your class in English," I said.

She grimaced ruefully. "No, I'm at the bottom of my class, because I don't know English grammar," she said. I think that disclosure is about the best commentary on what adults consider education.

Indifferent scholars who, under discipline, scrape through college or university and become unimaginative teachers, mediocre doctors, and incompetent lawyers would possibly be good mechanics or excellent bricklayers or first-rate policemen.

We have found that the boy who cannot or will not learn to read until he is, say, fifteen is always a boy with a mechanical bent who later on becomes a good engineer or electrician. I should not dare dogmatize about girls who never go to lessons, especially to mathematics and physics. Often such girls spend much time with needlework, and some, later on in life, take up dressmaking and designing. It is an absurd curriculum that makes a prospective dressmaker study quadratic equations or Boyle's Law.

Caldwell Cook wrote a book called *The Play Way*, in which he told how he taught English by means of play. It was a fascinating book, full of good things, yet I think it was only a new way of bolstering the theory that learning is of the utmost importance. Cook held that learning was so important that the pill should be sugared with play. This notion that unless a child is learning something the child is wasting his time is nothing less than a curse—a curse that blinds thousands of teachers and most school inspectors. Fifty years ago the watchword was "Learn through doing." Today the watchword is "Learn through playing." Play is thus used only as a means to an end, but to what good end I do not really know.

If a teacher sees children playing with mud, and he thereupon improves the shining moment by holding forth about river-bank erosion, what end has he in view? What child cares about river erosion? Many so-called educators believe that it does not matter what a child learns as long as he is *taught* something. And, of course, with schools as they are—just mass-production factories—what can a teacher do but teach something and come to believe that teaching, in itself, matters most of all?

When I lecture to a group of teachers, I commence by saying that I am not going to speak about school subjects or discipline or classes. For an hour my audience listens in rapt silence; and after the sincere applause, the chairman announces that I am ready to answer questions. At least three-quarters of the questions deal with subjects and teaching.

I do not tell this in any superior way. I tell it sadly to show how the classroom walls and the prisonlike buildings narrow the teacher's outlook, and prevent him from seeing the true essentials of education. His work deals with the part of a child that is above the neck; and perforce, the emotional, vital part of the child is foreign territory to him.

I wish I could see a bigger movement of rebellion among our younger teachers. Higher education and university degrees do not make a scrap of difference in confronting the evils of society. A learned neurotic is not any different than an unlearned neurotic.

In all countries, capitalist, socialist, or communist, elaborate schools are built to educate the young. But all the wonderful labs and workshops do nothing to help John or Peter or Ivan surmount the emotional damage and the social evils bred by the pressure on him from his parents, his schoolteachers, and the pressure of the coercive quality of our civilization.

What Happens to Summerhill Graduates

A parent's fear of the future affords a poor prognosis for the health of his children. This fear, oddly enough, shows itself in the desire that his children should learn more than he has learned. This kind of parent is not content to leave Willie to learn to read when he wants to, but nervously fears that Willie will be a failure in life unless he is pushed. Such parents cannot wait for the child to go at his own rate. They ask, If my son cannot read at twelve, what chance has he of success in life? If he cannot pass college entrance exams at eighteen, what is there for him but an unskilled job? But I have learned to wait and watch a child make little or no progress. I never doubt that in the end, if not molested or damaged, he will succeed in life.

Of course, the philistine can say, "Humph, so you call a truck driver a success in life!" My own criterion of success is *the ability to work joyfully and to live positively.* Under that definition most pupils in Summerhill turn out to be successes in life.

Tom came to Summerhill at the age of five. He left at seventeen, without having in all those years gone to a single lesson. He spent much time in the workshop making things. His father and mother trembled with apprehension about his future. He never showed any desire to learn to read. But one night when he was nine, I found him in bed reading *David Copperfield.*

"Hullo," I said, "who taught you to read?"

"I taught myself."

Some years later, he came to me to ask, "How do you add a half and two-fifths?" and I told him. I asked if he wanted to know any more. "No thanks," he said.

Later on, he got work in a film studio as a camera boy. When he was learning his job, I happened to meet his boss at a dinner party, and I asked how Tom was doing.

"The best boy we ever had," the employer said. "He never walks—he runs. And at week-ends, he is a damned nuisance, for on Saturdays and Sundays he won't stay away from the studio."

There was Jack, a boy who could not learn to read. No one could teach Jack. Even when he asked for a reading lesson, there was some hidden obstruction that kept him from distinguishing between *b* and *p*, *l* and *k*. He left school at seventeen without the ability to read.

Today, Jack is an expert toolmaker. He loves to talk about metalwork. He can read now; but so far as I know, he mainly reads articles about mechanical things—and sometimes he reads works on psychology. I do not think he has ever read a novel; yet he speaks perfectly grammatical English, and his general knowledge is remarkable. An American visitor, knowing nothing of his story, said to me, "What a clever lad Jack is!"

Diane was a pleasant girl who went to lessons without much interest. Her mind was not academic. For a long time, I wondered what she would do. When she left at sixteen, any inspector of schools would have pronounced her a poorly educated girl. Today, Diane is demonstrating a new kind of cookery in London. She is highly skilled at her work; and more important, she is *happy* in it.

One firm demanded that its employees should have at least passed the standard college entrance exams. I wrote to the head of the firm concerning Robert, "This lad did not pass any exams, for he hasn't got an academic head. But he has got guts." Robert got the job.

Winifred, aged thirteen, a new pupil, told me that she hated all subjects, and shouted with joy when I told her she was free to do exactly as she liked. "You don't even have to come to school if you don't want to," I said.

She set herself to have a good time, and she had one—for a few weeks. Then I noticed that she was bored.

"Teach me something," she said to me one day; "I'm bored stiff."

"Righto!" I said cheerfully, "what do you want to learn?"

"I don't know," she said.

"And I don't either," said I, and I left her.

Months passed. Then she came to me again. "I am going to pass the college entrance exams," she said, "and I want lessons from you."

Every morning she worked with me and other teachers, and she worked well. She confided that the subjects did not interest her much, but the aim *did* interest her. Winifred found herself by being allowed to be herself.

It is interesting to know that free children take to mathematics. They find joy in geography and in history. Free children cull from the offered subjects only those which interest them. Free children spend most time at other interests—woodwork, metalwork, painting, reading fiction, acting, playing out fantasies, playing jazz records.

Tom, aged eight, was continually opening my door and asking, "By the way, what'll I do now?" No one would tell him what to do.

Six months later, if you wanted to find Tom you went to his room. There you always found him in a sea of paper sheets. He spent hours making maps. One day a professor from the University of Vienna visited Summerhill. He ran across Tom and asked him many questions. Later the professor came to me and said, "I tried to examine that boy on geography, and he talked of places I never heard of."

But I must also mention the failures. Barbel, Swedish, fifteen, was with us for about a year. During all that time, she found no work that interested her. She had come to Summerhill too late. For ten years of her life, teachers had been making up her mind for her. When she came to Summerhill, she had already lost all initiative. She was bored. Fortunately, she was rich and had the promise of a lady's life.

I had two Yugoslavian sisters, eleven and fourteen. The school failed to interest them. They spent most of their time making rude remarks about me in Croatian. An unkind friend used to translate these for me. Success would have been miraculous in this case, for the only common speech we had was art and music. I was very glad when their mother came for them.

Over the years we have found that Summerhill boys who are going in for engineering do not bother to take the matriculation exams. They go straight to practical training centers. They have a tendency to see the world before they settle down to university work. One went around the world as a ship's steward. Two boys took up coffee farming in Kenya. One boy went to Australia, and one even went to remote British Guiana.

Derrick Boyd is typical of the adventurous spirit that a free education encourages. He came to Summerhill at the age of eight and left after passing his university exams at eighteen. He wanted to be a doctor, but his father could not afford to send him to the university at the time. Derrick thought he would fill in the waiting time by seeing the world. He went to the London docks and spent two days trying to get a job—any job—even as a stoker. He was told that too many real sailors were unemployed, and he went home sadly.

Soon a schoolmate told him of an English lady in Spain who wanted a chauffeur. Derrick seized the chance, went to Spain, built the lady a house or enlarged her existing house, drove her all over Europe, and then went to the university. The lady decided to help him with his university fees. After two years, the lady asked him to take a year off to drive her to Kenya and build her a house there. Derrick finished his medical studies in Capetown.

Larry, who came to us about the age of twelve, passed university exams at sixteen and went out to Tahiti to grow fruit. Finding this a poorly paid occupation, he took to driving a taxi. Later he went to New Zealand, where I understand he did all sorts of jobs, including driving another taxi. He then entered

Brisbane University. Some time ago, I had a visit from the dean of that university, who gave an admiring account of Larry's doings. "When we had vacation and the students went home," he said, "Larry went out to work as a laborer at a sawmill." He is now a practicing physician in Essex, England.

Some old boys, it is true, have not shown enterprise. For obvious reasons, I cannot describe them. Our successes are always those whose homes were good. Derrick and Jack and Larry had parents who were completely in sympathy with the school, so that the boys never had that most tiresome of conflicts: Which is right, home or school?

Has Summerhill produced any geniuses? No, so far no geniuses; perhaps a few creators, not famous as yet; a few bright artists; some clever musicians; no successful writer that I know of; an excellent furniture designer and cabinetmaker; some actors and actresses; some scientists and mathematicians who may yet do original work. I think that for our numbers—about forty-five pupils in the school at one time—a generous proportion has gone into some kind of creative or original work.

However, I have often said that one generation of free children does not prove anything much. Even in Summerhill some children get a guilty conscience about not learning enough lessons. It could not be otherwise in a world in which examinations are the gateways to some professions. And also, there is usually an Aunt Mary who exclaims, "Eleven years old and you can't read properly!" The child feels vaguely that the whole outside environment is anti-play and pro-work.

Speaking generally, the method of freedom is almost sure with children under twelve, but children over twelve take a long time to recover from a spoon-fed education.

Self-Government

Summerhill is a self-governing school, democratic in form. Everything connected with social, or group, life, including punishment for social offenses, is settled by vote at the Saturday night General School Meeting.

Each member of the teaching staff and each child, regardless of his age, has one vote. My vote carries the same weight as that of a seven-year-old.

One may smile and say, "But your voice has more value, hasn't it?" Well, let's see. Once I got up at a meeting and proposed that no child under sixteen should be allowed to smoke. I argued my case: a drug, poisonous, not a real appetite in children, but mostly an attempt to be grown up. Counterarguments were thrown across the floor. The vote was taken. I was beaten by a large majority.

The sequel is worth recording. After my defeat, a boy of sixteen proposed that no one under twelve should be allowed to smoke. He carried his motion. However, at the following weekly meeting, a boy of twelve proposed the repeal of the new smoking rule, saying, "We are all sitting in the toilets smoking on the sly just like kids do in a strict school, and I say it is against the whole idea of Summerhill." His speech was cheered, and that meeting repealed the law. I hope I have made it clear that my voice is not always more powerful than that of a child.

Once, I spoke strongly about breaking the bedtime rules, with the consequent noise and the sleepy heads that lumbered around the next morning. I proposed that culprits should be fined all their pocket money for each offense. A boy of fourteen proposed that there should be a penny reward per hour for everyone staying up after his or her bedtime. I got a few votes, but he got a big majority.

Summerhill self-government has no bureaucracy. There is a different chairman at each meeting, appointed by the previous chairman, and the secretary's job is voluntary. Bedtime officers are seldom in office for more than a few weeks.

Our democracy makes laws—good ones, too. For example, it is forbidden to bathe in the sea without the supervision of lifeguards, who are always staff members. It is forbidden to climb on the roofs. Bedtimes must be kept or there is an automatic fine. Whether classes should be called off on the Thursday or on the Friday preceding a holiday is a matter for a show of hands at a General School Meeting.

The success of the meeting depends largely on whether the chairman is weak or strong, for—to keep order among forty-five vigorous children is no easy task. The chairman has power to fine noisy citizens. Under a weak chairman, the fines are much too frequent.

The staff takes a hand, of course, in the discussions. So do I; although there are a number of situations in which I must remain neutral. In fact, I have seen a lad charged with an offense get away with it on a complete alibi, although he had privately confided to me that he had committed the offense. In a case like this, I must always be on the side of the individual.

I, of course, participate like anyone else when it comes to casting my vote on any issue or bringing up a proposal of my own. Here is a typical example. I once raised the question of whether football should be played in the lounge. The lounge is under my office, and I explained that I disliked the noise of football while I was working. I proposed that indoor football be forbidden. I was supported by some of the girls, by some older boys, and by most of the staff. But my proposal was not carried, and that meant my continuing to put up with the noisy scuffle of feet below my office. Finally, after much public disputation at several meetings, I did carry by majority approval the abolition of football in the lounge. And this is the way the minority generally gets its rights in our school democracy; it keeps demanding them. This applies to little children as much as it does to adults.

On the other hand, there are aspects of school life that do not come under the self-government regime. My wife plans the arrangements for bedrooms, provides the menu, sends out and pays bills. I appoint teachers and ask them to leave if I think they are not suitable.

The function of Summerhill self-government is not only to make laws but to discuss social features of the community as well. At the beginning of each term, rules about bedtime are made by vote. You go to bed according to your age. Then questions of general behavior come up. Sports committees have to be elected, as well as an end-of-term dance committee, a theater committee, bedtime officers, and downtown officers who report any disgraceful behavior out of the school boundaries.

The most exciting subject ever brought up is that of food. I have more than once waked up a dull meeting by proposing that second helpings be abolished. Any sign of kitchen favoritism in the matter of food is severely handled. But when the kitchen brings up the question of wasting food, the meeting is not much interested. The attitude of children toward food is essentially a personal and self-centered one.

In a General School Meeting, all academic discussions are avoided. Children are eminently practical and theory bores them. They like concreteness, not abstraction. I once brought forward a motion that swearing be abolished by law, and I gave my reason. I had been showing a woman around with her little boy, a prospective pupil. Suddenly from upstairs came a very strong adjective. The mother hastily gathered up her son and went off in a hurry. "Why," I asked at a meeting, "should my income suffer because some fathead swears in front of a prospective parent? It isn't a moral question at all; it is purely financial. You swear and I lose a pupil."

My question was answered by a lad of fourteen. "Neill is talking rot," he said. "Obviously, if this woman was shocked, she didn't believe in Summerhill. Even if she had enrolled her boy, the first time he came home saying damn or hell, she would have taken him out of here." The meeting agreed with him, and my proposal was voted down.

A General School Meeting often has to tackle the problem of bullying. Our community is pretty hard on bullies; and I notice that the school government's bullying rule has been underlined on the bulletin board: "*All cases of bullying will be severely dealt with.*" Bullying is not so rife in Summerhill, however, as in strict schools, and the reason is not far to seek. Under adult discipline, the child becomes a hater. Since the child cannot express his hatred of adults with impunity, he takes it out on smaller or weaker boys. But this seldom happens in Summerhill. Very often, a charge of bullying when investigated amounts to the fact that Jenny called Peggy a lunatic.

Sometimes a case of stealing is brought up at the General School Meeting. There is never any punishment for stealing, but there is always reparation. Often children will come to me and say, "John stole some coins from David. Is this a case for psychology, or shall we bring it up?"

If I consider it a case for psychology, requiring individual attention, I tell them to leave it to me. If John is a happy, normal boy who has stolen something inconsequential, I allow charges to be brought against him. The worst that happens is that he is docked all of his pocket money until the debt is paid.

How are General School Meetings run? At the beginning of each term, a chairman is elected for one meeting only. At the end of the meeting he appoints his successor. This procedure is followed throughout the term. Anyone who has a grievance, a charge, or a suggestion, or a new law to propose brings it up.

Here is a typical example: Jim took the pedals from Jack's bicycle because his own cycle is in disrepair, and he wanted to go away with some other boys for a week-end trip. After due consideration of the evidence, the meeting decides that Jim must replace the pedals, and he is forbidden to go on the trip.

The chairman asks, "Any objections?"

Jim gets up and shouts that there jolly well are! Only his adjective isn't exactly "jolly." "This isn't fair!" he cries. "I didn't know that Jack ever used his old crock of a bike. It has been kicking about among the bushes for days. I don't mind shoving his pedals back, but I think the punishment unfair. I don't think I should be cut out of the trip."

Follows a breezy discussion. In the debate, it transpires that Jim usually gets a weekly allowance from home, but the allowance hasn't come for six weeks, and he hasn't a bean. The meeting votes that the sentence be quashed, and it is duly quashed.

But what to do about Jim? Finally it is decided to open a subscription fund to put Jim's bike in order. His schoolmates chip in to buy him pedals for his bike, and he sets off happily on his trip.

Usually, the School Meeting's verdict is accepted by the culprit. However, if the verdict is unacceptable, the defendant may appeal, in which case the chairman will bring up the matter once again at the very end of the meeting. At such an appeal, the matter is considered more carefully, and generally the original verdict is tempered in view of the dissatisfaction of the defendant. The children realize that if the defendant feels he has been unfairly judged, there is a good chance that he actually has been.

No culprit at Summerhill ever shows any signs of defiance or hatred of the authority of his community. I am always surprised at the docility our pupils show when punished.

One term, four of the biggest boys were charged at the General School Meeting with doing an illegal thing—selling various articles from their wardrobes. The law forbidding this had been passed on the ground that such practices are unfair to the parents who buy the clothes and unfair as well to the school, because when children go home minus certain wearing apparel, the parents blame the school for carelessness. The four boys were punished by being kept on the grounds for four days and being sent to bed at eight each night. They accepted the sentence without a murmur. On Monday night, when everyone had gone to the town movies, I found Dick, one of the culprits, in bed reading.

"You are a chump," I said. "Everyone has gone to the movies. Why don't you get up?"

"Don't try to be funny," he said.

This loyalty of Summerhill pupils to their own democracy is amazing. It has no fear in it, and no resentment. I have seen a boy go through a long trial for some antisocial act, and I have seen him sentenced. Often, the boy who has just been sentenced is elected chairman for the next meeting.

The sense of justice that children have never ceases to make me marvel. And their administrative ability is great. As education, self-government is of infinite value.

Certain classes of offenses come under the automatic fine rule. If you ride another's bike without permission, there is an automatic fine of sixpence. Swearing in town (but you can swear as much as you like on the school grounds), bad behavior in the movies, climbing on roofs, throwing food in the dining room—these and other infractions of rules carry automatic fines.

Punishments are nearly always fines: hand over pocket money for a week or miss a movie.

An oft-heard objection to children acting as judges is that they punish too harshly. I find it not so. On the contrary, they are very lenient. On no occasion has there been a harsh sentence at Summerhill. And invariably the punishment has some relation to the crime.

Three small girls were disturbing the sleep of others. Punishment: they must go to bed an hour earlier every night for a week. Two boys were accused of throwing clods at other boys. Punishment: they must cart clods to level the hockey field.

Often the chairman will say, "The case is too silly for words," and decide that nothing should be done.

When our secretary was tried for riding Ginger's bike without permission, he and two other members of the staff who had also ridden it were ordered to push each other on Ginger's bike ten times around the front lawn.

Four small boys who climbed the ladder that belonged to the builders who were erecting the new workshop were ordered to climb up and down the ladder for ten minutes straight.

The meeting never seeks advice from an adult. Well, I can remember only one occasion when it was done. Three girls had raided the kitchen larder. The meeting fined them their pocket money. They raided the kitchen again that night and the meeting fined them a movie. They raided it once more, and the meeting was graveled what to do. The chairman consulted me. "Give them tuppence reward each," I suggested. "What? Why, man, you'll have the whole school raiding the kitchen if we do that." "You won't," I said. "Try it."

He tried it. Two of the girls refused to take the money; and all three were heard to declare that they would never raid the larder again. They didn't—for about two months.

Priggish behavior at meetings is rare. Any sign of priggishness is frowned upon by the community. A boy of eleven, a strong exhibitionist, used to get up and draw attention to himself by making long involved remarks of obvious irrelevance. At least he tried to, but the meeting shouted him down. The young have a sensitive nose for insincerity.

At Summerhill we have proved, I believe, that self-government works. In fact, the school that has no self-government should not be called a progressive school. It is a compromise school. You cannot have freedom unless children feel completely free to govern their own social life. When there is a boss, there is no real freedom. This applies even more to the benevolent boss than to the disciplinarian. The child of spirit can rebel against the hard boss, but the soft boss merely makes the child impotently soft and unsure of his real feelings.

Good self-government in a school is possible only when there is a sprinkling of older pupils who like a quiet life and fight the indifference or opposition of the gangster age. These older youngsters are often outvoted, but it is they who really believe in and want self-government. Children up to, say, twelve, on the other hand, will not run good self-government on their own, because they have not reached the social age. Yet at Summerhill, a seven-year-old rarely misses a General Meeting.

One spring we had a spate of bad luck. Some community-minded seniors had left us after passing their college entrance exams, so that there were very few seniors left in the school. The vast majority of the pupils were at the gangster stage and age. Although they were social in their speeches, they were not old enough to run the community well. They passed any amount of laws and then forgot them and broke them. The few older pupils left were, by some chance, rather individualist, and tended to live their own lives in their own groups, so that the staff was figuring too prominently in attacking the breaking of the school rules. Thus it came about that at a General School Meeting I felt compelled to launch a vigorous attack on the seniors for being not antisocial but asocial, breaking the bedtime rules by sitting up far too late and taking no interest in what the juniors were doing in an antisocial way.

Frankly, younger children are only mildly interested in government. Left to themselves, I question whether younger children would ever form a government. Their values are not our values, and their manners are not our manners.

Stern discipline is the easiest way for the adult to have peace and quiet. Anyone can be a drill sergeant. What the ideal alternative method of securing a quiet life is I do not know. Our Summerhill trials and errors certainly fail to give the adults a quiet life. On the other hand they do not give the children an overnoisy life. Perhaps the ultimate test is happiness. By this criterion, Summerhill has found an excellent compromise in its self-government.

Our law against dangerous weapons is likewise a compromise. Air guns are forbidden. The few boys who want to have air guns in the school hate the law; but in the main, they conform to it. When they are a minority, children do not seem to feel so strongly as adults do.

In Summerhill, there is one perennial problem that can never be solved; it might be called the problem of *the individual vs. the community.* Both staff and pupils get exasperated when a gang of little girls led by a problem girl annoy some people, throw water on others, break the bedtime laws, and make themselves a perpetual nuisance. Jean, the leader, is attacked in a General Meeting. Strong words are used to condemn her misuse of freedom as license.

A visitor, a psychologist, said to me: "It is all wrong. The girl's face is an unhappy one; she has never been loved, and all this open criticism makes her feel more unloved than ever. She needs love, not opposition."

"My dear woman," I replied, "we *have* tried to change her with love. For weeks, we rewarded her for being antisocial. We have shown her affection and tolerance, and she has not reacted. Rather, she has looked on us as simpletons, easy marks for her aggression. We cannot sacrifice the entire community to one individual."

I do not know the complete answer. I know that when Jean is fifteen, she will be a social girl and not a gang leader. I pin my faith on public opinion. No child will go on for years being disliked and criticized. As for the condemnation by the school meeting, one simply cannot sacrifice other children to one problem child.

Once, we had a boy of six who had a miserable life before he came to Summerhill. He was a violent bully, destructive and full of hate. The four- and five-year-olds suffered and wept. The community had to do something to protect them; and in doing so, it had to be against the bully. The mistakes of two parents could not be allowed to react on other children whose parents had given them love and care.

On a very few occasions, I have had to send a child away because the others were finding the school a hell because of him. I say this with regret, with a vague feeling of failure, but I could see no other way.

Have I had to alter my views on self-government in these long years? On the whole, no. I could not visualize Summerhill without it. It has always been popular. It is our show piece for visitors. But that, too, has its drawbacks, as when a girl of fourteen whispered to me at a meeting, "I meant to bring up about girls blocking the toilets by putting sanitary napkins in them, but look at all these visitors." I advised her to damn the visitors and bring the matter up—which she did.

The educational benefit of practical civics cannot be overemphasized. At Summerhill, the pupils would fight to the death for their right to govern themselves. In my opinion, one weekly General School Meeting is of more value than a week's curriculum of school subjects. It is an excellent theater for practicing public speaking, and most of the children speak well and without self-consciousness. I have often heard sensible speeches from children who could neither read nor write.

I cannot see an alternative method to our Summerhill democracy. It may be a fairer democracy than the political one, for children are pretty charitable to each other, and have no vested interests to speak of. Moreover, it is a more genuine democracy because laws are made at an open meeting, and the question of uncontrollable elected delegates does not arise.

After all, it is the broad outlook that free children acquire that makes self-government so important. Their laws deal with essentials, not appearances. The laws governing conduct in the town are the compromise with a less free civilization. "Downtown"—the outside world—wastes its precious energy in worrying over trifles. As if it matters in the scheme of life whether you wear dressy clothes or say hell. Summerhill, by getting away from the outward nothings of life, can have and does have a community spirit that is in advance of its time. True, it is apt to call a spade a damn shovel, but any ditchdigger will tell you with truth that a spade *is* a damn shovel.

Work

In Summerhill, we used to have a community law that provided that every child over twelve and every member of the staff must do two hours of work each week on the grounds. The pay was a token pay of a nickel an hour. If you did not work, you were fined a dime. A few, teachers included, were content to pay the fines. Of those who worked, most had their eyes on the clock. There was no play component in the work, and therefore the work bored everyone. The law was re-examined, and the children abolished it by an almost unanimous vote.

A few years ago, we needed an infirmary in Summerhill. We decided to build one ourselves—a proper building of brick and cement. None of us had ever laid a brick, but we started in. A few pupils helped to dig the foundations and knocked down some old brick walls to get the bricks. But the children demanded payment. We refused to pay wages. In the end, the infirmary was built by the teachers and visitors. The job was just too dull for children, and to their young minds the need for the sanatorium too remote. They had no self-interest in it. But some time later when they wanted a bicycle shed, they built one all by themselves without any help from the staff.

I am writing of children—not as we adults think they should be—but as they really are. Their community sense—their sense of social responsibility—does not develop until the age of eighteen or more. Their interests are immediate, and the future does not exist for them.

I have never yet seen a lazy child. What is called laziness is either lack of interest or lack of health. A healthy child cannot be idle; he has to be doing something all day long. Once I knew a very healthy lad who was considered a lazy fellow. Mathematics

100

did not interest him, but the school curriculum demanded that he learn mathematics. Of course, he didn't want to study mathematics, and so his math teacher thought he was lazy.

I read recently that if a couple who were out for an evening were to dance every dance they would be walking twenty-five miles. Yet they would feel little or no fatigue because they would be experiencing pleasure all evening long—assuming that their steps agreed. So it is with a child. The boy who is lazy in class will run miles during a football game.

I find it impossible to get youths of seventeen to help me plant potatoes or weed onions, although the same boys will spend hours souping up motor engines, or washing cars, or making radio sets. It took me a long time to accept this phenomenon. The truth began to dawn on me one day when I was digging my brother's garden in Scotland. I didn't enjoy the job, and it came to me suddenly that what was wrong was that I was digging a garden that meant nothing to me. And my garden means nothing to the boys, whereas their bikes or radios mean a lot to them. True altruism is a long time in coming, and it never loses its factor of selfishness.

Small children have quite a different attitude toward work than teen-agers have. Summerhill juniors, ranging from age three to eight, will work like Trojans mixing cement or carting sand or cleaning bricks; and they will work with no thought of reward. They identify themselves with grownups and their work is like a fantasy worked out in reality.

However, from the age of eight or nine until the age of nineteen or twenty, the desire to do manual labor of a dull kind is just not there. This is true of most children; there are individual children, of course, who remain workers from early childhood right on through life.

The fact is that we adults exploit children far too often. "Marion, run down to the mail box with this letter." Any child hates to be made use of. The average child dimly realizes that he is fed and clothed by his parents without any effort on his part. He feels that such care is his natural right, but he realizes that on the other hand he is expected and obliged to do a hundred menial tasks and many disagreeable chores, which the parents themselves evade.

I once read about a school in America that was built by the pupils themselves. I used to think that this was the ideal way. It isn't. If children built their own school, you can be sure that some gentleman with a breezy, benevolent authority was standing by, lustily shouting encouragement. When such authority is not present, *children simply do not build schools.*

My own opinion is that a sane civilization would not ask children to work until at least the age of eighteen. Most boys and girls would do a lot of work before they reached eighteen, but such work would be play for them, and probably uneconomical work from the viewpoint of the parents. I feel depressed when I think of the gigantic amount of work students have to do to prepare for exams. I understand that in prewar Budapest nearly fifty per cent of the students broke down physically or psychologically after their matriculation exams.

The reason we here in Summerhill keep getting such good reports about the industrious performance of our old pupils on responsible jobs is that these boys and girls have lived out their self-centered fantasy stage in Summerhill. As young adults they are able to face the realities of life without any unconscious longing for the play of childhood.

Play

Summerhill might be defined as a school in which play is of the greatest importance. Why children and kittens play I do not know. I believe it is a matter of energy.

I am not thinking of play in terms of athletic fields and organized games; I am thinking of play in terms of fantasy. Organized games involve skill, competition, teamwork; but children's play usually requires no skill, little competition, and hardly any teamwork. Small children will play gangster games with shooting or sword play. Long before the motion picture era, children played gang games. Stories and movies will give a direction to some kind of play, but the fundamentals are in the hearts of all children of all races.

At Summerhill the six-year-olds play the whole day long—play with fantasy. To a small child, reality and fantasy are very close to each other. When a boy of ten dressed himself up as a ghost, the little ones screamed with delight; they knew it was only Tommy; they had seen him put on that sheet. But as he advanced on them, they one and all screamed in terror.

Small children live a life of fantasy and they carry this fantasy over into action. Boys of eight to fourteen play gangsters and are always bumping people off or flying the skies in their wooden airplanes. Small girls also go through a gang stage, but it does not take the form of guns and swords. It is more personal. Mary's gang objects to Nellie's gang, and there are rows and hard words. Boys' rival gangs are only play enemies. Small boys are thus more easy to live with than small girls.

I have not been able to discover where the borderline of fantasy begins and ends. When a child brings a doll a meal on a tiny toy plate, does she really believe for the moment that the doll is alive? Is a rocking horse a real horse? When a boy cries "Stick 'em up" and then fires, does he think or feel that his is a real gun? I am inclined to think that children do imagine that their toys are real, and only when some insensitive adult butts in and reminds them of their fantasy do they come back to earth with a plop. No sympathetic parent will ever break up a child's fantasy.

Boys do not generally play with girls. Boys play gangsters, and play tag; they make huts in trees; they dig holes and trenches.

Girls seldom organize any play. The time-honored game of playing teacher or doctor is unknown among free children, for they feel no need to mimic authority. Smaller girls play with dolls; but older girls seem to get the most fun out of contact with people, not things.

We have often had mixed hockey teams. Card games and other indoor games are usually mixed.

Children love noise and mud; they clatter on stairs; they shout like louts; they are unconscious of furniture. If they are playing a game of touch, they would walk over the Portland Vase if it happened to be in their way—walk over it without seeing it.

Mothers, too often, do not play enough with their babies. They seem to think that putting a soft teddy bear in the carriage with the baby solves things for an hour or two, forgetting that babies want to be tickled and hugged.

Granting that childhood is playhood, how do we adults generally react to this fact? We *ignore* it. We forget all about it—because play, to us, is a waste of time. Hence we erect a large city school with many rooms and expensive apparatus for teaching; but more often than not, all we offer to the play instinct is a small concrete space.

One could, with some truth, claim that the evils of civilization are due to the fact that no child has ever had enough play. To put it differently, every child has been hothoused into an adult long before he has reached adulthood.

The adult attitude toward play is quite arbitrary. We, the old, map out a child's timetable: Learn from nine till twelve and then an hour for lunch; and again lessons until three. If a free child were asked to make a timetable, he would almost certainly give to play many periods and to lessons only a few.

Fear is at the root of adult antagonism to children's play. Hundreds of times I have heard the anxious query, "But if my boy plays all day, how will he ever learn anything; how will he ever pass exams?" Very few will accept my answer, "If your child plays all he wants to play, he will be able to pass college entrance exams after two years' intensive study, instead of the usual five, six, or seven years of learning in a school that discounts play as a factor in life."

But I always have to add, "That is—if he ever *wants* to pass the exams!" He may want to become a ballet dancer or a radio engineer. She may want to be a dress designer or a children's nurse.

Yes, fear of the child's future leads adults to deprive children of their right to play. There is more in it than that, however. There is a vague moral idea behind the disapproval of play, a suggestion that being a child is not so good, a suggestion voiced in the admonition to young adults, "Don't be a kid."

Parents who have forgotten the yearnings of their childhood—forgotten how to play and how to fantasy—make poor parents. When a child has lost the ability to play, he is psychically dead and a danger to any child who comes in contact with him.

Teachers from Israel have told me of the wonderful community centers there. The school, I'm told, is part of a community whose primary need is hard work. Children of ten, one teacher told me, weep if—as a punishment—they are not allowed to dig the garden. If I had a child of ten who wept because he was forbidden to dig potatoes, I should wonder if he were mentally defective. Childhood is playhood; and any community system that ignores that truth is educating in a wrong way. To me the Israeli method is sacrificing young life to economic needs. It may be necessary; but I would not dare to call that system ideal community living.

It is intriguing, yet most difficult, to assess the damage done to children who have not been allowed to play as much as they wanted to. I often wonder if the great masses who watch professional football are trying to live out their arrested play interest by identifying with the players, playing by proxy as it were. The majority of our Summerhill graduates does not attend football matches, nor is it interested in pageantry. I believe few of them would walk very far to see a royal procession. Pageantry has a childish element in it; its color, formalism, and slow movement have some suggestion of toyland and dressed-up dolls. That may be the reason that women seem to love pageantry more than men do. As people get older and more sophisticated, they seem to be attracted less and less by pageantry of any kind. I doubt if generals and politicians and diplomats get anything out of state processions except boredom.

There is some evidence that children brought up freely and with the maximum of play do not tend to become mass-minded. Among old Summerhillians, the only ones who can easily and enthusiastically cheer in a crowd are the ones who came from the homes of parents with Communist leanings.

Theater

During the winter, Sunday night at Summerhill is acting night. The plays are always well attended. I have seen six successive Sunday nights with a full dramatic program. But sometimes after a wave of dramatics there will not be a performance for a few weeks.

The audience is not too critical. It behaves well—much better than most London audiences do. We seldom have catcalls or feet thumping or whistling.

The Summerhill theater is a converted squash-rackets court, which holds about a hundred people. It has a movable stage; that is, it is made of boxes that can be piled up into steps and platforms. It has proper lighting with elaborate dimming devices and spotlights. There is no scenery—only gray curtains. When the cue is *Enter villagers through gap in hedge*, the actors push the curtain aside.

The tradition of the school is that only plays written in Summerhill are performed. And the unwritten code is that a play written by a teacher is performed only if there is a dearth of children's plays. The cast makes its own costumes, too, and these are usually exceptionally well done. Our school dramas tend toward comedy and farce rather than tragedy; but when we have a tragedy, it is well done—sometimes beautifully done.

Girls write plays more than boys do. Small boys often produce their own plays; but usually the parts are not written out. They hardly need to be, for the main line of each character is always "Stick 'em up!" In these plays the curtain is always rung down on a set of corpses, for small boys are by nature thorough and uncompromising.

Daphne, a girl of thirteen, used to give us Sherlock Holmes plays. I remember one about a constable who ran away with the sergeant's wife. With the aid of the sleuth and, of course, "My Dear Watson" the sergeant tracked the wife to the constable's lodgings. There a remarkable sight met their eyes. The constable lay on a sofa with his arm around the faithless wife, while a bevy of demimonde women danced sinuous dances in the middle of the room. *The constable was in evening dress.* Daphne always brought high life into her dramas.

Girls of fourteen or so sometimes write plays in verse, and these are often good. Of course, not all the staff and children write plays.

There is a strong aversion to plagiarism. When, some time ago, a play was dropped from the program and I had to write one hastily as a stopgap, I wrote on the theme of one of W. W. Jacob's stories. There was an outcry of "Copycat! Swindler!"

Summerhill children do not like dramatized stories. Nor do they want the usual highbrow stuff so common in other schools. Our crowd never acts Shakespeare; but sometimes I write a Shakespearean skit as, for example, Julius Caesar with an American gangster setting—the language a mixture of Shakespeare and a detective story magazine.

Mary brought the house down when as Cleopatra she stabbed everyone on the stage; and then, looking at the blade of her knife, read aloud the words "stainless steel," and plunged the knife into her breast.

The acting ability of the pupils is of a high standard. Among Summerhill pupils there is no such thing as stage fright. The little children are a delight to see; they live their parts with complete sincerity. The girls act more readily than the boys. Indeed, boys under ten seldom act at all except in their own gangster plays; and some children never get to act nor have any desire to do so.

We discovered in our long experience that the worst actor is he who acts in life. Such a child can never get away from himself and is self-conscious on the stage. Perhaps self-conscious is the wrong term, for it means being conscious that others are conscious of you.

Acting is a necessary part of education. It is largely exhibitionism; but at Summerhill when acting becomes only exhibitionism, an actor is not admired.

As an actor, one must have a strong power of identifying oneself with others. With adults, this identification is never unconscious; adults know they are play-acting. But I question if small children really do know. Quite often, when a child enters and his cue is, "Who are you?" instead of answering, "I am the abbey ghost!" he will answer, "I'm Peter."

In one of the plays written for the very youngest, there was a dinner scene with real viands. It took the prompter some time and concern to get the actors to move on to the next scene. The children went on tucking in the food with complete indifference to the audience.

Acting is one method of acquiring self-confidence. But some children who never act tell me that they hate the performances because they feel so inferior. Here is a difficulty for which I have found no solution. Such a child generally finds another line of endeavor in which he can show superiority. The difficult case is that of the girl who loves acting but can't act. It says much for the good manners of the school that such a girl is seldom left out of a cast.

Boys and girls of thirteen and fourteen refuse to take any part that involves making love, but the small children will play any part easily and gladly. The seniors who are over fifteen will play love parts if they are comedy parts. Only one or two seniors will take a serious love part. Love parts cannot be well played until one has experienced love. Yet children who have never known grief in real life may act splendidly in a sorrowful part. I have seen Virginia break down at rehearsals and weep while playing a sad part. That is accounted for by the fact that every child has known grief in imagination. In fact, death enters early into every child's fantasies.

Plays for children ought to be at the level of the children. It is wrong to make children do classical plays which are far away from their real fantasy life. Their plays, like their reading, should be for their age. Summerhill children seldom read Scott or Dickens or Thackeray, because today's children belong to an age of movies. When a child goes to the movies, he gets a story as long as *Westward Ho* in an hour and a quarter—a story that would take him days to read, a story without all the dull descriptions of people and landscapes. So in their plays children do not want a story of Elsinore; they want a story of their own environment.

Although Summerhill children perform the plays that they themselves write, they nevertheless, when given the opportunity, respond enthusiastically to really fine drama. One winter I read a play to the seniors once a week. I read all of Barrie, Ibsen, Strindberg, Chekhov, some of Shaw and Galsworthy, and some modern plays like *The Silver Cord* and *The Vortex*. Our best actors and actresses liked Ibsen.

The seniors are interested in stage techniques and take an original view of it. There is a time-honored trick in playwriting of never allowing a character to leave the stage without his making an excuse for doing so. When a dramatist wanted to get rid of the father so that the wife and daughter could tell each other what an ass he was, old father obligingly got up, and remarking, "Well, I'd better go and see if the gardener has planted those cabbages," he shuffled out. Our young Summerhill playwrights have a more direct technique. As one girl said to me, "In real life you go out of a room without saying anything about why you are going." You *do*, and you do on the Summerhill stage, too.

Summerhill specializes in a certain branch of dramatic art which we call spontaneous acting. I set acting tasks like the following: *Put on an imaginary overcoat; take it off again and hang it on a peg. Pick up a bunch of flowers and find a thistle among them. Open a telegram that tells you your father (or mother) is dead. Take a hasty meal at a railroad restaurant and be on tenterhooks lest the train leave without you.*

Sometimes the acting is a "talkie." For example, I sit down at a table and announce that I am an immigration officer at Harwich. Each child has to have an imaginary passport and must be prepared to answer my questions. That is good fun.

Again, I am a film producer interviewing a prospective cast, or a businessman seeking a secretary. Once I was a man who had advertised for an amanuensis. None of the children knew what the word meant. One girl acted as if it meant a manicurist and this afforded some good comedy.

Spontaneous acting is the creative side of a school theater—is the vital side. Our theater has done more for creativity than anything else in Summerhill. Anyone can act in a play, but everyone cannot write a play. The children must realize, even if dimly, that their tradition of performing only original, home-grown plays encourages creativity rather than reproduction and imitation.

Dancing and Music

On with the dance—but it must be danced according to the rules. And the strange thing is that the crowd will accept the rules as a crowd, while at the same time the individuals composing the crowd may be unanimous in hating the rules.

To me a London ballroom symbolizes what England is. Dancing, which should be an individual and creative pleasure, is reduced to a stiff walk. One couple dances just like another couple. Crowd conservatism prevents most dancers from being original. Yet the joy of dancing is the joy of invention. When invention is left out, dancing becomes mechanical and dull. English dancing fully expresses the English fear of emotion and originality.

If there is no room for freedom in such a pleasure as dancing, how can we expect to find it in the more serious aspects of life? If one dare not invent his own dance steps, it is unlikely that he will be tolerated if he dares to invent his own religious, educational, or political steps!

At Summerhill, every program includes dances. These are always arranged and performed by the girls, and they do them well. They do not dance to classical music; it is always jazz. We had one ballet to Gershwin's *An American in Paris* music. I wrote the story and the girls interpreted it in dance. I have seen worse dances on the London stage.

Dancing serves as an excellent outlet for unconscious sex interest. I say *unconscious* because a girl may be a beauty, but if she is a bad dancer, she will not have many dance partners.

Nearly every night our private living room is filled with children. We often play phonograph records and here disagreements arise. The children want Duke Ellington and Elvis Presley and I hate the stuff. I like Ravel and Stravinsky and Gershwin. Sometimes I get fed up with jazz and lay down the law, saying that since it is my room I'll play what I want to play.

The *Rosenkavalier* trio or the *Meistersinger* quintet will clear the room. But then, few children like classical music or classical paintings. We make no attempt to lead them to higher tastes— whatever that may mean.

Actually, it does not matter to one's happiness in life whether one loves Beethoven or hot jazz. Schools would have more success if they included jazz in the curriculum and left out Beethoven. At Summerhill, three boys, inspired by jazz bands, took up musical instruments. Two of them bought clarinets and one chose a trumpet. On leaving school, they all went to study at the Royal Academy of Music. Today, they are all playing in orchestras which play classical music exclusively. I like to think that the reason for this advance in musical taste is that when they were at Summerhill each was permitted to hear Duke Ellington *and* Bach, or any other composer for that matter.

Sports and Games

In most schools, sports are compulsory. Even the watching of matches is compulsory. In Summerhill, games are, like lessons, optional.

One boy was in the school for ten years and didn't play a game, and he was never asked to play a game. But most of the children love games. The juniors do not organize games. They play gangsters or red Indians; they build tree huts and do all the things that small children usually do. Not having reached the cooperative stage, they should not have games organized for them. Organized play and sports come naturally at the right time.

At Summerhill, our chief games are hockey in the winter and tennis in the summer. One difficulty with children is to get good teamwork in tennis doubles. They take teamwork for granted in hockey; but often two tennis players act as individuals instead of as a single unit. Teamwork comes more easily about the age of seventeen.

Swimming is very popular with all ages. The beach at Sizewell is not a good beach for children, for the tide seems always to be full. The long stretches of sand with rocks and pools so dear to children are not to be found on our coast.

We have no artificial gymnastics in the school, nor do I think them necessary. The children get all the exercise they need in their games, swimming, dancing, and cycling. I question if free children would go to a gym class. Our indoor games are table tennis, chess, cards.

The younger children have a paddling pool, a sand pit, a seesaw and swings. The sand pit is always filled with grubby children on a warm day; and the younger ones are always complaining that the bigger children come and use their sand pit. It appears that we shall have to have a sand pit for the seniors. The sand and mud-pie era lives on longer than we thought it did.

We have had debates and wranglings about our inconsistency in giving prizes for sports. The inconsistency lies in our resolute refusal to introduce prizes or marks into the school curriculum. The argument against rewards is that a thing should be done for its own sake, not for the reward; and that is indeed true. So we are sometimes asked why it is right to give a prize for tennis, but wrong to give one for geography. I suppose the answer is that a game of tennis is naturally competitive and consists in beating the other fellow. The study of geography is not. If I know geography, I don't really care if the other fellow knows less or more geography than I do. I know that children *want* prizes for games, and they don't want them for school subjects—at least not in Summerhill. In Summerhill, at any rate, we do not turn our sports winners into heroes. Because Fred is captain of the hockey team does not give his voice added weight in a General School Meeting.

Sports in Summerhill are in their proper place. A boy who never plays a game is never looked down upon and never considered an inferior. "Live and let live" is a motto that finds its ideal expression when children are free to be themselves. I, myself, have little interest in sports, but I am keenly interested in good sportsmanship. If Summerhill teachers had urged, "Come on, lads, get on the field!" sports in Summerhill would have become a perverted thing. Only under freedom to play or not to play can one develop true sportsmanship.

The Future of Summerhill

Now that I am in my seventy-sixth year, I feel that I shall not write another book about education, for I have little new to say. But what I have to say has something in my favor; I have not spent the last forty years writing down *theories* about children. Most of what I have written has been based on observing children, living with them. True, I have derived inspiration from Freud, Homer Lane, and others; but gradually, I have tended to drop theories when the test of reality proved them invalid.

It is a queer job that of an author. Like broadcasting, an author sends out some sort of message to people he does not see, people he cannot count. My public has been a special one. What might be called the official public knows me not. The British Broadcasting Company would never think of inviting me to broadcast on education. No university, my own of Edinburgh included, would ever think of offering me an honorary degree. When I lecture to Oxford and Cambridge students, no professor, no don comes to hear me. I think I am rather proud of these facts, feeling that to be acknowledged by the officials would suggest that I was out-of-date.

At one time, I resented the fact that *The London Times* would never publish any letter I sent in; but today, I feel their refusal is a compliment.

I am not claiming that I have gotten away from the wish for recognition; yet age brings changes—especially changes in values. Recently I lectured to seven hundred Swedes, packing a hall built for six hundred, and I had no feeling of elation or conceit. I thought I was really indifferent until I asked myself the question, "How would you have felt if the audience had consisted of ten?" The answer was "damned annoyed," so that if positive pride is lacking, negative chagrin is not.

Ambition dies with age. Recognition is a different matter. I do not like to see a book with the title of, say, *The History of Progressive Schools* when such a book ignores my work. I have never yet met anyone who was honestly indifferent to recognition.

There is a comical aspect about age. For years I have been trying to reach the young—young students, young teachers, young parents—seeing age as a brake on progress. Now that I am old—one of the Old Men I have preached against so long—I feel differently. Recently, when I talked to three hundred students in Cambridge, I felt myself the youngest person in the hall. I *did*. I said to them: "Why do you need an old man like me to come and tell *you* about freedom?" Nowadays, I do not think in terms of youth and age. I feel that years have little to do with one's thinking. I know lads of twenty who are ninety, and men of sixty who are twenty. I am thinking in terms of freshness, enthusiasm, of lack of conservatism, of deadness, of pessimism.

I do not know if I have mellowed or not. I suffer fools less gladly than I used to do, am more irritated by boring conversations, and less interested in people's personal histories. But then, I've had far too many imposed on me these last thirty years. I also find less interest in things, and seldom want to buy anything. I haven't looked in a clothes shop window for years. And even my beloved tool shops in Euston Road do not attract me nowadays.

If I have now reached the stage when children's noise tires me more than it used to, I cannot say that age has brought impatience. I can still see a child do all the wrong things, live out all the old complexes, knowing that in good time the child will be a good citizen. Age lessens fear. But age also lessens courage. Years ago, I could easily tell a boy who threatened to jump from a high window if he did not get his own way, to go on and jump. I am not so sure I could do so today.

A question that is often put to me is, "But isn't Summerhill a one-man show? Could it carry on without you?" Summerhill is by no means a one-man show. In the day-by-day working of the school, my wife and the teachers are just as important as I am. *It is the idea of noninterference with the growth of the child and non-pressure on the child that has made the school what it is.*

Is Summerhill known throughout the world? Hardly. And only to a comparative handful of educators. Summerhill is best known in Scandinavia. For thirty years, we have had pupils from Norway, Sweden, Denmark—sometimes twenty at a time. We have also had pupils from Australia, New Zealand, South Africa, and Canada. My books have been translated into many languages, including Japanese, Hebrew, Hindustani, and Gujarati. Summerhill has had some influence in Japan. Over thirty years ago, we had a visit from Seishi Shimoda, an outstanding educator. All his translations of my books have sold rather well; and I hear that teachers in Tokyo meet to discuss our methods. Mr. Shimoda again spent a month with us in 1958. A principal of a school in the Sudan tells me that Summerhill is of great interest to some teachers there.

I put down these facts about translations, visits, and correspondence without illusions. Stop a thousand people in Oxford Street and ask them what the word Summerhill conveys to them. Very likely none of them would know the name. One should cultivate a sense of humor about one's importance or lack of it.

I do not think that the world will use the Summerhill method of education for a very long time—if it ever uses it. The world may find a better way. Only an empty windbag would assume that his work is the last word on the subject. The world *must* find a better way. For politics will not save humanity. It never has done so. Most political newspapers are bristling with hate, hate all the time. Too many are socialistic because they hate the rich instead of loving the poor.

How can we have happy homes with love in them when the home is a tiny corner of a homeland that shows hate socially in a hundred ways? You can see why I cannot look upon education as a matter of exams and classes and learning. The school evades the basic issue: All the Greek and math and history in the world will not help to make the home more loving, the child free from inhibitions, the parent free of neurosis.

The future of Summerhill itself may be of little import. But the future of the Summerhill idea is of the greatest importance to humanity. New generations must be given the chance to grow in freedom. The bestowal of freedom is the bestowal of love. And only love can save the world.

The Free Child

There are so few self-regulated babies in the world that any attempt to describe them must be tentative. The observed results so far suggest the beginnings of a new civilization, more profoundly changed in character than any new society promised by any kind of political party.

Self-regulation implies a belief in the goodness of human nature; a belief that there is not, and never was, original sin.

No one has ever seen a completely self-regulated child. Every child living has been molded by parents, teachers, and society. When my daughter Zoë was two, a magazine, *Picture Post*, published an article about her with photographs, saying that in their opinion, she of all the children of Britain had the best chance of being free. It was not entirely true, for she lived, and lives, in a school among many children who were not self-regulated. These other children had been more or less conditioned; and since character-molding must lead to fear and hate, Zoë found herself in contact with some children who were anti-life.

She was brought up with no fear of animals. Yet one day, when I stopped the car at a farm and said, "Come on, let's see the moo cows," she suddenly looked afraid and said, "No, no, moo cows eat you." A child of seven, who had not been brought up with self-regulation, had told her so. True, the fear lasted only for a week or two. A subsequent tale of tigers lurking in the bushes also had only a short life of influence.

It would seem that a self-regulated child is capable of overcoming the influences of conditioned children in a comparatively short time. Zoë's acquired fears and repressed interests never lasted long; but no one can say what permanent harm, if any, these acquired fears have already wrought on her character.

Scores of outsiders from all over the world have said of Zoë, "Here is something quite new, a child of grace and balance and happiness, at peace with her surroundings, not at war." It is true; she is, as near as can be in a neurotic society, the natural child who seems automatically to know the boundary between freedom and license.

One of the dangers of having a self-regulated child is that adults will show so much interest in her that she gets too much in the center of the picture. It is likely that in a community of self-regulated children, where all were natural and free, no single child would stand out. None would be encouraged to show off. And then, there would not be the jealousy that other children exhibit when faced with a free child who does not have their inhibitions.

Compared with her friend Ted, Zoë as a young child was supple and free of limb. You lifted her and her body was as relaxed as that of a kitten; but poor Ted lifted like a sack of potatoes. He could not relax; his reactions were all defensive and resisting; he was anti-life in every direction.

I prophesy that self-regulated children will not go through that unpleasant phase. I cannot see why they will ever need to. For if they have no feeling of being tied and restricted by parents when they are in the nursery, I cannot see any reason why rebellion against parents should arise later. Even in semifree homes, the equality between parents and children is often so good that the rebellious striving to get free from the parents does not arise.

Self-regulation means the right of a baby to live freely, without outside authority in things psychic and somatic. It means that the baby feeds when it is hungry; that it becomes clean in habits only when it wants to; that it is never stormed at nor spanked; that it is always loved and protected.

It all sounds easy and natural and fine, yet it is astounding how many young parents, keen on the idea, manage to misunderstand it. Tommy, aged four, bangs the notes of a neighbor's piano with a wooden mallet. His fond parents look on with a triumphant smile which means, "Isn't self-regulation wonderful?"

Other parents think that they ought never to put their baby of eighteen months to bed, because that would be interfering with nature. No, baby must be allowed to stay up; when he is tired out, mother will carry him to his cot. What actually happens is that baby gets increasingly tired and cross. He cannot say that he wants to go to sleep, because he cannot verbalize his need. Usually, the weary and disappointed mother lifts him and carries him screaming to bed. Another young couple came to me rather apologetically, and asked if it would be wrong for them to put up a fireguard in a baby's nursery. All these illustrations show that any idea, old or new, is dangerous, if not combined with common sense.

Only a fool in charge of young children would allow unbarred bedroom windows or an unprotected fire in the nursery. Yet, too often, young enthusiasts for self-regulation come to my school as visitors, and exclaim at our lack of freedom in locking poison in a lab closet, or our prohibition about playing on the fire escape. The whole freedom movement is marred and despised because so many advocates of freedom have not got their feet on the ground.

One such protested to me recently because I shouted sternly at a problem boy of seven who was kicking my office door. His idea was that I should smile and tolerate the noise until the child should live out his desire to bang doors. It is true that I spent a good few years of my life patiently tolerating the destructive behavior of problem children, but I did this as their psychological doctor and not as their fellow citizen.

If a young mother thinks that her child of three should be allowed to paint the front door with red ink on the ground that he is thereby expressing himself freely, she is incapable of grasping what self-regulation means.

I remember sitting with a friend in the Covent Garden theater. During the first ballet, a child in front of us talked loudly to her father. At the end of the ballet, I found other seats. My companion said to me, "What would you do if one of your kids from Summerhill did that?"

"Tell him to shut up," I said.

"You wouldn't need to," said my friend; "he just wouldn't act that way." And I don't think any of them would.

Once a woman brought her girl of seven to see me. "Mr. Neill," she said, "I have read every line you have written; and even before Daphne was born, I had decided to bring her up exactly along your lines."

I glanced at Daphne who was standing on my grand piano with her heavy shoes on. She made a leap for the sofa and nearly went through the springs. "You see how natural she is," said the mother. "The Neillian child!" I fear that I blushed.

It is this distinction between freedom and license that many parents cannot grasp. In the disciplined home, the children have *no* rights. In the spoiled home, they have *all* the rights. The proper home is one in which children and adults have equal rights. And the same applies to school.

It must be emphasized again and again that freedom does not involve spoiling the child. If a baby of three wants to walk over the dining table, you simply tell him he must not. He must obey, that's true. But on the other hand, you must obey him when necessary. I get out of small children's rooms if they tell me to get out.

There has to be a certain amount of sacrifice on the part of the adult if children are to live according to their inner nature. Healthy parents come to some sort of a compromise agreement; unhealthy parents either become violent or they spoil their children by allowing them to have all the social rights.

In practice, the divergence of interests between parents and children can be mitigated, if not solved, by an honest give and take. Zoë respected my desk, and showed no compulsion to play with my typewriter and papers. In turn, I respected her nursery and playthings.

Children are very wise and soon accept social laws. They should not be exploited as they too often are. Too often a parent calls out, "Jimmy, get me a glass of water," when the child is intent on an engrossing game.

A great amount of naughtiness is due to the wrong method of handling. Zoë, when a little over a year old, went through a period of great interest in my glasses, snatching them off my nose to see what they were like. I made no protest, showed no annoyance by look or tone of voice. She soon lost interest in my glasses and never touched them. No doubt, if I had sternly told her not to—or worse, spanked her little hand—her interest in my glasses would have survived, mingled with fear of me and rebellion against me.

My wife let her play with breakable ornaments. The child handled them carefully and seldom broke anything. She found things out for herself. Of course, there is a limit to self-regulation. We cannot allow a baby of six months to discover that a lighted cigarette burns painfully. It is wrong to shout in alarm in such a case; the right thing to do is to remove the danger without any fuss.

Unless a child is mentally defective, he will soon discover what interests him. Left free from excited cries and angry voices, he will be unbelievably sensible in his dealing with material of all kinds. The harassed mother standing at the gas stove, frantic about what the children are doing, is she who has never trusted her children in their activities. "Go and see what baby is doing and tell him he mustn't" is still a phrase applying to many homes today.

When a mother writes asking me what she should do with children messing things up while she is busy cooking the dinner, I can only reply that perhaps she has brought them up that way.

One couple read some of my books and were conscience-stricken when they thought of the harm they had done in bringing up their children. They summoned the family to a conference and said, "We have brought you up all wrong. From now on, you are free to do what you like." I forget how much they said the breakage bill came to, but I can recall that they had to summon a second conference and rescind the previous motion.

The usual argument against freedom for children is this: Life is hard, and we must train the children so that they will fit into life later on. We must therefore discipline them. If we allow them to do what they like, how will they ever be able to serve under a boss? How will they compete with others who have known discipline? How will they ever be able to exercise self discipline?

People who protest the granting of freedom to children and use this argument do not realize that they start with an unfounded, unproved assumption—the assumption that a child will not grow or develop unless forced to do so. Yet the entire thirty-nine years of experience of Summerhill disproves this assumption. Take, among one hundred others, the case of Mervyn. He attended Summerhill for ten years, between the ages of seven to seventeen. During those ten years, Mervyn never attended a single class. At age seventeen, he hardly knew how to read. Yet when Mervyn left school and decided to become an instrument maker, he quickly taught himself how to read and absorbed in a short time through self-study all the technical knowledge he needed. Through his own efforts, he made himself ready for his apprenticeship. Today, this same chap is thoroughly literate, commands a good salary, and is a leader in his community. As to self-discipline, Mervyn built a good part of his house with his own hands and he is bringing up a fine family of three boys from the fruits of his daily labors.

Similarly, each year boys and girls at Summerhill who up to then have rarely studied, decide to enter college; and of their own accord, they then begin the long and tiresome grind of preparing themselves for college entrance examinations. Why do they do it?

The common assumption that good habits that have not been forced into us during early childhood can never develop in us later on in life is an assumption we have been brought up on and which we unquestioningly accept merely because the idea has never been challenged. I deny this premise.

Freedom is necessary for the child because only under freedom can he grow in his natural way—the good way. I see the results of bondage in new pupils coming from prep schools and convents. They are bundles of insincerity, with an unreal politeness and phony manners.

Their reaction to freedom is rapid and tiresome. For the first week or two, they open doors for the teachers, call me "Sir," and wash carefully. They glance at me with "respect," which is easily recognized as fear. After a few weeks of freedom, they show what they really are. They become impudent, unmannerly, unwashed. They do all the things they have been forbidden to do in the past: they swear, they smoke, they break things. And all the time, they have a polite and insincere expression in their eyes and in their voices.

It takes at least six months for them to lose their insincerity. After that, they also lose their deference to what they regarded as authority. In just about six months, they are natural, healthy kids who say what they think without fluster or hate. When a child comes to freedom young enough, he does not have to go through this stage of insincerity and acting. The most striking thing about Summerhill is this absolute sincerity among the pupils.

This business of being sincere in life and to life is a vital one. It is really the most vital one in the world. If you have sincerity, all other things will be added to you. Everyone realizes the value of sincerity in, say, acting. We expect sincerity from our politicians (such is the optimism of mankind), from our judges and magistrates, teachers and doctors. Yet we educate our children in such a way that they dare not be sincere.

Possibly the greatest discovery we have made in Summerhill, is that a child is born a sincere creature. We set out to let children alone so that we might discover what they were like. It is the only possible way of dealing with children. The pioneer school of the future must pursue this way if it is to contribute to child knowledge and, more important, to child happiness.

The aim of life is happiness. The evil of life is all that limits or destroys happiness. Happiness always means goodness; unhappiness at its extreme limits means Jew-baiting, minority torture, or war.

But I grant that sincerity has its awkward moments. As when recently a girl of three looked at a bearded visitor and said, "I don't think I like your face." The visitor rose to the occasion. "But I like yours," he said, and Mary smiled.

No, I won't argue for freedom for children. One half-hour spent with a free child is more convincing than a book of arguments. Seeing is believing.

To give a child freedom is not easy. It means that we refuse to teach him religion, or politics, or class consciousness. A child cannot have real freedom when he hears his father thunder against some political group, or hears his mother storm against the servant class. It is well-nigh impossible to keep children from adopting our attitude to life. The son of a butcher will not be likely to preach vegetarianism—that is, unless fear of his father's authority drives him into opposition.

The very nature of society is inimical to freedom. Society— the crowd—is conservative and hateful toward new thought.

Fashion typifies the crowd's dislike of freedom. The crowd demands uniformity. In town I am a crank because I wear sandals; in my village I would be a crank if I wore a tall hat. Few men dare to depart from *the correct thing*.

The law in England—the law of the crowd—forbids the buying of cigarettes after eight o'clock at night. I cannot think of one individual who approves of this law. As individuals, we calmly accept crowd rulings that are stupid.

Few individuals would care to take the responsibility of hanging a murderer, or of sending a criminal to the living death we call prison. The crowd can retain such barbarities as capital punishment and our prison system, for the crowd has no conscience. The crowd cannot think, it can only feel. To the crowd, the criminal is a danger; the easiest way of protection is to kill the danger or lock it up. Our obsolete criminal code is based fundamentally on fear; and our suppressive system of education is also fundamentally based on fear—fear of the new generation.

Sir Martin Conway in his delightful book, *The Crowd in Peace and War*, points out that the crowd likes old men. In war, it chooses old generals; in peace, it prefers old doctors. The crowd clings to the old because it fears the young.

The instinct of self-preservation in a crowd sees in the new generation a danger—the danger of having a new, rival crowd grow up—a crowd that may conceivably destroy the old crowd. In the smallest crowd of all—the family—freedom is denied to the young for the same reason. The adults cling to old values— old *emotional* values. There is no logical basis for a father's prohibiting his twenty-year-old daughter from smoking. The prohibition springs from emotional sources, from conservative sources. At the back of the prohibition is fear, *What may she do next?* The crowd is the guardian of morality. The adult fears to give freedom to the young because he fears that the young may do indeed all the things that he, the adult, has wanted to do. The eternal imposition on children of adult conceptions and values is a great sin against childhood.

To give freedom is to allow the child to live his own life. Thus expressed, it seems simple. Only our disastrous habit of teaching and molding and lecturing and coercing renders us incapable of realizing the simplicity of true freedom.

What is the child's reaction to freedom? Children clever and children not-so-clever gain something that they never had before—a something that is almost indefinable. Its chief outer sign is a great increase in sincerity and charity, plus a lessening of aggression. When children are not under fear and discipline, they are not patently aggressive. Only once in thirty-eight years at Summerhill have I seen a fight with bloody noses. We always have a small bully around—for no amount of freedom at school can completely counteract the influence of a bad home. Character acquired in the first months or years of life can be modified by freedom, but it can never be completely changed. The archenemy of freedom is fear. If we tell children about sex, will they not become licentious? If we do not censor plays, will the people not become immoral?

The adults who fear that youth will be corrupted are those who are themselves corrupt—just as it is the dirty-minded people who demand that we should all wear two-piece bathing suits. If a man is shocked by anything, it is by the thing that he is most interested in. The prude is the libertine without the courage to face his naked soul.

But freedom means the conquest of ignorance. A free people would need no censor of plays or of costumes. For a free people would have no interest in shocking things, because a free people could not be shocked. Summerhill pupils are unshockable—not because they are advanced in sin—but because they have lived out their interests in shocking things and have no more use for them as subjects of conversation or wit.

People are always saying to me, "But how will your free children ever adapt themselves to the drudgery of life?" I hope that these free children will be pioneers in *abolishing* the drudgery of life.

We must allow the child to be selfish—ungiving—free to follow his own childish interests through his childhood. When the child's individual interests and his social interests clash, the individual interests should be allowed precedence. The whole idea of Summerhill is release: allowing a child to live out his natural interests.

A school should make a child's life a game. I do not mean that the child should have a path of roses. Making it all easy for the child is fatal to the child's character. But life itself presents so many difficulties that the artificially made difficulties which we present to children are unnecessary.

I believe that to impose anything by authority is wrong. The child should not do anything until he comes to the opinion—his own opinion—that it should be done. The curse of humanity is the external compulsion, whether it comes from the Pope or the state or the teacher or the parent. It is fascism in toto.

Most people demand a god; how can it be otherwise when the home is ruled by tin gods of both sexes, gods who demand perfect truth and moral behavior? Freedom means doing what you like, so long as you don't interfere with the freedom of others. The result is self-discipline.

In our educational policy as a nation, we refuse to let live. We persuade through fear. But there is a great difference between compelling a child to cease throwing stones and compelling him to learn Latin. Throwing stones involves others; but learning Latin involves only the boy. The community has the right to restrain the antisocial boy because he is interfering with the rights of others; but the community has no right to compel a boy to learn Latin—for learning Latin is a matter for the individual. Forcing a child to learn is on a par with forcing a man to adopt a religion by act of Parliament. And it is equally foolish.

I learned Latin as a boy—rather I was given Latin books to learn from. As a boy, I could never learn the stuff because my interests were elsewhere. At the age of twenty-one, I found that I could not enter the university without Latin. In less than a year, I learned enough Latin to pass the entrance exam. Self-interest made me learn Latin.

Every child has the right to wear clothes of such a kind that it does not matter a brass farthing if they get messy or not. Every child has the right to freedom of speech. I have had many years of hearing adolescent children let off all the *bloodies* and *hells* they had been forbidden to say in the nursery.

The surprising thing is that, with millions reared in sex hate and fear, the world is not more neurotic than it is. To me this means that natural humanity has the innate power of finally overcoming the evils that are imposed on it. There is a slow trend to freedom, sexual and otherwise. In my boyhood, a woman went bathing wearing stockings and a long dress. Today, women show legs and bodies. Children are getting more freedom with every generation. Today, only a few lunatics put cayenne pepper on a baby's thumb to stop sucking. Today, only a few countries beat their children in school.

Freedom works slowly; it may take several years for a child to understand what it means. Anyone who expects quick results is an incurable optimist. And freedom works best with clever children. I should like to be able to say that, since freedom primarily touches the emotions, all kinds of children—intelligent and dull—react equally to freedom. I cannot say it.

One sees the difference in the matter of lessons. Every child under freedom plays most of the time for years; but when the time comes, the bright ones will sit down and tackle the work necessary to master the subjects covered by government exams. In a little over two years, a boy or girl will cover the work that disciplined children take eight years to cover.

The orthodox teacher holds that exams will be passed only if discipline keeps the candidate's nose to the grindstone. Our results prove that with bright pupils that is a fallacy. Under freedom, it is only the bright ones who can concentrate on intensive study, a most difficult thing to do in a community in which so many counterattractions are going on.

I know that under discipline comparatively poor scholars pass exams, but I wonder what becomes of the passers later on in life. If all schools were free and all lessons were optional, I believe that children would find their own level.

I can hear some harassed mother, busy with her cooking— while her baby is crawling about and upsetting things—ask with irritation, "What's all this self-regulation anyway? All very well for rich women with nurses; but for the likes of me, just words and confusion."

Another might cry, "I'd like to, but how do I start? What books can I read on the subject?"

The answer is that there are no books, no oracles, no authorities. All there is, is a very small minority of parents and doctors and teachers who believe in the personality and the organism we call a child, and who are determined to do nothing to warp that personality and stiffen its body by wrong interference. We are all nonauthoritarian seekers after the truth about humanity. All we can offer is an account of our observations of young children brought up in freedom.

Love and Approval

The happiness and well-being of children depend on the degree of love and approval we give them. We must be on the child's side. Being on the side of the child is giving love to the child—not possessive love—not sentimental love—just behaving to the child in such a way that the child feels you love him and approve of him.

It can be done. I know scores of parents who are on the side of their children, demanding nothing in return, and therefore getting a lot. They realize that children are not little adults.

When a son of ten writes home, "Dear Mommy, please send me fifty cents. Hope you are well. Love to Daddy," the parents smile, knowing that that is what a child of ten writes if he is sincere and not afraid to express himself. The wrong type of parent sighs at such a letter, and thinks: *The selfish little beast, always asking for something.*

The right parents of my school never ask how their children are getting along; they see for themselves. The wrong type keep asking me impatient questions: *Can he read yet? When is he ever going to be tidy? Does she ever go to lessons?*

It is all a matter of faith in children. Some have it; most haven't it. And if you do not have this faith, the children feel it. They feel that your love cannot be very deep, or you would trust them more. When you approve of children you can talk to them about anything and everything, for approval makes many inhibitions fly away.

But the question arises, Is it possible to approve of children if you do not approve of yourself? If you are not aware of yourself, you cannot approve of yourself. In other words, the more conscious you are of yourself and your motives, the more likely you are to be an approver of yourself.

I express the earnest hope, then, that more knowledge of oneself and of child nature will help parents to keep their children free from neurosis. I repeat that parents are spoiling their children's lives by forcing on them outdated beliefs, outdated manners, outdated morals. They are sacrificing the child to the past. This is especially true of those parents who impose authoritative religion on their children just as it was once imposed on them.

I know well that the most difficult thing in the world is to renounce things we consider important, but it is only through renunciation that we find life, find progress, find happiness. Parents must renounce. They must renounce hate that is disguised as authority and criticism. They must renounce the intolerance that is the outcome of fear. They must renounce old morals and mob verdicts.

Or more simply, the parent must become an individual. He must know where he really stands. It is not easy. For a man is not just himself. He is a combination of everyone he has met, and he retains many of their values. Parents impose the authority of their own parents because every man has in him his own father, every woman her own mother. It is the imposing of this rigid authority that breeds hate, and with it, problem children. It is the opposite of giving the child approval.

Many a girl has said to me, "I can't do a thing to please Mommy. She can do everything better than I can, and she flies into a temper if I make a mistake in sewing or knitting."

Children do not need teaching as much as they need love and understanding. They need approval and freedom to be naturally good. It is the genuinely strong and loving parent who has the most power to give children freedom to be good.

The world is suffering from too much condemnation, which is really a fancier way of saying that the world is suffering from too much hate. It is the parents' hate that makes a child a problem, just as it is society's hate that makes the criminal a problem. Salvation lies in love, but what makes it difficult is that no one can *compel* love.

The parent of the problem child must sit down and ask himself or herself these questions: *Have I shown real approval of my child? Have I shown trust in him? Have I shown understanding?* I am not theorizing. I know that a problem child can come to my school and become a happy, normal child. I know that the chief ingredients in the curing process are the showing of approval, of trust, of understanding.

Approval is just as necessary for normal children as for problem children. The one commandment that every parent and teacher must obey is this: *Thou shalt be on the child's side.* The obeying of this commandment is what makes Summerhill a successful school. For we are definitely on the child's side—and the child knows it unconsciously.

I do not say that we are a crowd of angels. There are times when we adults make a fuss. If I should be painting a door and Robert came along and threw mud on my fresh paint, I would swear at him heartily, because he has been one of us for a long time and what I say to him does not matter. But suppose Robert had just come from a hateful school and his mud slinging was his attempt to fight authority, I would join with him in his mud slinging because his salvation is more important than the door. I know that I must stay on his side while he lives out his hate in order for him to become social again. It isn't easy. I have stood by and seen a boy treat my precious lathe badly. I knew that if I protested he would at once identify me with his stern father who always threatened to beat him if he touched his tools.

The strange thing is that you can be on the child's side even though you sometimes swear at him. If you are on the side of the child, the child realizes it. Any minor disagreement you may have about potatoes or scratched tools does not disturb the fundamental relationship. When you treat a child without bringing in authority and morality, the child feels that you are on his side. In his previous life, authority and morality were like policemen who restricted his activities.

When a girl of eight passes me and says in passing, "Neill is a silly fool," I know that that is just her negative way of expressing her love, of telling me that she feels at ease. Children do not so much love as they want to be loved. To every child, adult approval means love; whereas disapproval means hate. The attitude of the children to the Summerhill staff is quite like the attitude of the children to me. The children feel that the staff is on their side all the time.

I have already mentioned the sincerity of free children. This sincerity is the result of their being approved of. They have no artificial standards of behavior to live up to, no taboos to restrain them. They have no necessity to live a life that is a lie.

New pupils, coming from schools where they had to respect authority, address me as *Mister*. Only when they discover that I am not an authority do they drop the *Mister* and call me Neill. They never seek to get my personal approval—only the approval of the whole school community. But in the days when I was a village schoolmaster in Scotland, any child would gladly stay behind to help me clean up the classroom or prune a hedge outdoors, seeking—insincerely—my approval because I was the boss.

No child in Summerhill ever does anything to gain my approval, although visitors may conclude otherwise when they see some boys and girls helping me clear weeds. The motive for the work has nothing to do with me personally. In this particular instance the children were weeding because a General-Meeting law made by the pupils themselves provided that everyone over twelve was obliged to do two hours of work each week in the garden. This law was later rescinded.

In any society, however, there is a natural desire for approval. The criminal is he who has lost the desire for approval by the large part of society, or rather the criminal is he who has been forced to change the desire for approval into its opposite, the contempt for society. The criminal is always Egoist No. 1: *Let me get rich quick and to hell with society.* Prison sentences merely armor his egoism. A prison term merely compels the criminal to become a lone bird, brooding on himself and the horrible society that punishes him. Punishment and prison sentences cannot reform the criminal, because to him they are only a proof of society's hate. Society eliminates the chance of his becoming social in order to gain the approval of others. This insane, inhuman prison system stands condemned because it does not touch anything of psychological value in the prisoner.

Hence I say that the first essential in any reform school is the chance of social approval. So long as boys have to salute overseers, stand in military lines, jump up if the superintendent enters the room, there is no real freedom, and therefore no chance of social approval. Homer Lane found that when a new boy came to the *Little Commonwealth*, he sought the approval of his fellows, generally using the technique he had used in his slum street: he boasted of his misdeeds, of his cleverness in lifting from shops, of his prowess in dodging policemen. When he found he was boasting to youths who had got over that form of seeking social approval, the newcomer was nonplused, and he often contemptuously dismissed his new companions as sissies. Gradually his natural love of approval forced him to seek the approval of the people in his new environment. And, without any individual analysis by Lane, he adapted himself to his new companions. In a few months he was a social being.

*   *   *

Let me now address the ordinary, decent, sympathetic husband who comes home on the 5:20 train every evening.

I know you, John Brown. I know you want to love your children and be loved by them in return. I know that when your son of five wakens at two in the morning and yells persistently without any apparent cause, you will not feel much love for him at the moment. Be assured he has some reason for crying, even if you cannot immediately discover what it is. If you are angry, try not to show it. A man's voice is more terrifying to a baby than is that of a woman, and you never know what lifetime fears may be instilled into a baby by a loud angry voice at the wrong time.

"Don't lie in bed with the baby," says the pamphlet of instructions for parents. Forget it. Give the infant as much hugging and petting as you can.

Don't use your children as a means of showing off. In this be as careful of praising as of blaming. It is bad to rhapsodize about a child when he or she is present. *Oh, yes, Mary is getting on. First in her class last week. Clever girl.* Not that you should never praise your child. It is good to say to your son, *That's a very nice kite you have made,* but the praise in the service of impressing visitors is wrong. Young geese so easily stick out their necks like swans when admiration is floating around. It makes the child unrealistic about himself. You should never encourage your child in getting away from reality, in making a fantasy picture of himself. On the other hand, when the child fails, never rub it in. Even if the school report abounds with low marks, say nothing. And if Billy comes home weeping because he has been beaten in a fight, do not call him a sissy.

If you ever use the words *When I was your age . . .* you are making a dreadful mistake. The long and short of it is that you must approve your child as he is, and refrain from trying to make him in your own image.

My motto for the home, in education as in life, is this: *For heaven's sake, let people live their own lives.* It is an attitude that fits any situation.

This attitude is the only possible attitude that fosters toleration. It is strange that the word *toleration* has not occurred to me before. It is the proper word for a free school. We are leading the children along the way of being tolerant by showing *them* tolerance.

Obedience and Discipline

An impious question comes up: Why should a child obey? My answer is: He must obey to satisfy the adult's desire for power. Otherwise, why should a child obey?

"Well," you say, "he may get his feet wet if he disobeys the command to put on shoes; he may even fall over the cliff if he disobeys his father's shout." Yes, of course, the child should obey when it is a matter of life and death. But how often is a child punished for disobeying in matters of life and death? Seldom, if ever! He is generally hugged with a "My precious! Thank God, you're safe!" It is for *small things* that a child is usually punished.

Now it is possible to run a house where obedience is not required. If I say to a child, "Get your books and take a lesson in English," he may refuse if he is not interested in English. His disobedience merely expresses his own desires, which obviously do not intrude on or hurt anyone else. But if I say, "The center part of the garden is planted; no one is to run over it!" all the children accept what I say in much the same way that they accept Derrick's command, "Nobody is to use my ball unless they ask me first." For obedience should be a matter of give and take. Occasionally, at Summerhill, there is disobedience of a law passed in the General School Meeting. Then the children may themselves take action. However, in the main, Summerhill runs along without any authority or any obedience. Each individual is free to do what he likes *as long as he is not trespassing on the freedom of others*. And this is a realizable aim in any community.

Under self-regulation, there is no authority in the home. This means that there is no loud voice that declaims, "I say it! You must obey." In actual practice there is, of course, authority.

Such authority might be called protection, care, adult responsibility. Such authority sometimes demands obedience but at other times gives obedience. Thus I can say to my daughter, "You can't bring that mud and water into our parlor." That's no more than her saying to me, "Get out of my room, Daddy. I don't want you here now," a wish that I, of course, obey without a word.

Akin to punishment is the parental demand that a child should not bite off more than it can chew. Literally—for often a child's eye is bigger than his stomach and he will demand a plateful that he cannot consume. To force a child to finish what is on his plate is wrong. Good parenthood is the power of identifying oneself with a child, understanding his motives, realizing his limitations, without harboring ulterior motives or resentment.

One mother wrote me that she wanted her daughter to obey her. I was teaching her daughter to obey *herself*. The mother finds her disobedient, but I find her *always* obedient. Five minutes ago, she came into my room to argue about dogs and their training. "Buzz off," I said, "I'm busy writing." And she went out—without a word.

Obedience should be social courtesy. Adults should have no right to the obedience of children. It must come from within—not be imposed from without.

Discipline is a means to an end. The discipline of an army is aimed at making for efficiency in fighting. All such discipline subordinates the individual to the cause. In disciplined countries life is cheap.

There is, however, another discipline. In an orchestra, the first violinist obeys the conductor because he is as keen on a good performance as the conductor is. The private who jumps to attention does not, as a rule, care about the efficiency of the army. Every army is ruled mostly by fear, and the soldier knows that if he disobeys he will be punished. School discipline can be of the orchestra type when teachers are good. Too often it is of the army type. The same applies to the home. A happy home is like an orchestra and enjoys the same kind of team spirit. A miserable home is like a barracks that is ruled by hate and discipline.

The odd thing is that homes with team-spirit discipline often tolerate a school with army discipline. Boys are beaten by teachers—boys who are never beaten at home. A visitor from an older and wiser planet would consider the parents of this country morons if he were told that in some elementary schools, even today, small children are punished for mistakes in addition or in spelling. When humane parents protest against the beating discipline of the school and go to court about it, in most cases the law takes the side of the punishing teacher.

Parents could abolish corporal punishment tomorrow—if they wanted to. Apparently the majority do not want to. The system suits them. It disciplines their boys and girls. The hate of the child is cleverly directed to the punishing teacher and not to the parents who hire him to do the dirty work. The system suits these parents because they themselves were never allowed to live and love. They, too, were made slaves to group discipline, and the poor souls cannot visualize freedom.

It is true that there must be some discipline in the home. Generally, it is the type of discipline that safeguards the individual rights of each member of the family. For example, I do not allow my daughter, Zoë, to play with my typewriter. But in a happy family this kind of discipline usually looks after itself. Life is a pleasant give and take. Parents and children are chums, co-workers.

In the unhappy home, discipline is used as a weapon of hate, and obedience becomes a virtue. Children are chattels, things owned, and they must be a credit to their owners. I find that the parent who worries most about Billy's learning to read and write is one who feels a failure in life because of lack of educational attainment.

It is the self-disapproving parent who believes in strict discipline. The jovial man-about-town with a stock of obscene stories will sternly reprove his son for talking about excrement. The untruthful mother will spank her child for lying. I have seen a man, with pipe in mouth, whipping his son for smoking. I have heard a man say as he hit his son of twelve, "I'll teach you to swear, you little bastard." When I remonstrated, he said glibly, "It's different when I curse. He's just a kid."

Strict discipline in the home is always a projection of self-hate. The adult has striven for perfection in his own life, has failed miserably to reach it, and now attempts to find it in his children. And all because he cannot love. All because he fears pleasure as the very devil. That, of course, is why man *invented* the Devil—the fellow who has all the best tunes, who loves life and joy and sex. The aim of perfection is to conquer the Devil. And from this aim derive mysticism and irrationalism, religion and asceticism. From this derives, too, the crucifixion of the flesh in the form of beating and sexual abstinence and impotency.

It might justly be said that strict home discipline aims at castration in its widest sense, castration of life itself. No obedient child can ever become a free man or woman. No child punished for masturbation can ever be fully orgastically potent.

I have said that the parent wants the child to become what he or she has failed to become. There is more to it than that: every repressed parent is at the same time determined that his child shall not get more out of life than he, the parent, got. Unalive parents won't allow children to be alive. And such a parent always has an exaggerated fear of the future. Discipline, he thinks, will save his children. This same lack of confidence in his inner self makes him postulate an outside God who will *compel* goodness and truth. Discipline is thus a branch of religion.

The main difference between Summerhill and the typical school is that at Summerhill we have faith in the child's personality. We know that if Tommy wants to be a doctor, he will voluntarily study to pass the entrance examinations. The disciplined school is sure that Tommy will never be a doctor unless he is beaten or pressured or forced to study at prescribed hours.

I grant that in most cases it is easier to eliminate discipline from the school than from the home. In Summerhill, when a child of seven makes himself a social nuisance, the whole community expresses its disapproval. Since social approval is something that everyone desires, the child learns to behave well. No discipline is necessary.

In the home, where so many emotional factors and other circumstances enter, things are not so easy. The harassed housewife, cooking the dinner, cannot treat her fractious child with social disapproval. Nor can the tired father when he finds his new seedbed trampled upon. What I wish to emphasize is that *in a home where the child has had self-regulation from the start, ordinary demands for discipline do not arise!*

Some years ago, I visited my friend Wilhelm Reich in Maine. His son, Peter, was three years old. The lake at the doorstep was deep. Reich and his wife simply told Peter that he should not go near the water. Having had no hateful training and therefore having trust in his parents, Peter did not go near the water. The parents *knew* that they need not worry. Parents who discipline with fear and authority would have lived on that lakeshore with their nerves on edge. Children are so accustomed to being lied to that when mother says that water is dangerous, they simply don't believe her. They have a defiant wish to go to the water.

The disciplined child will express his hate of authority by annoying his parents. Indeed, much childish misbehavior is a visible proof of wrong treatment. The average child accepts the parental voice of knowledge—if there is love in the home. If there is hate in the home, he accepts nothing. Or he accepts things negatively: he is destructive and insolent and dishonest.

Children are wise. They will react to love with love, and will react to hate with hate. They will respond easily to discipline of the team type. I aver that badness is not basic in human nature any more than it is basic in rabbit nature or lion nature. Chain a dog and a good dog becomes a bad dog. Discipline a child and a good social child becomes a bad, insincere hater. Sad to say, most people are sure that a bad boy wants to be bad; they believe that with the help of God or a big stick, the child has the power of choosing to be good. And if he refuses to exercise this power, then they'll damn well see to it that he suffers for his contumaciousness.

In a way, the old school spirit symbolizes all that discipline stands for. The principal of a large boys' school said to me not long ago when I asked him what sort of boys he had, "The sort that goes out with neither ideas nor ideals. They would join up as cannon fodder in any war, never stopping to consider what the war was about and why they were fighting."

I haven't hit a child for nearly forty years. Yet as a young teacher, I used the strap vigorously without ever stopping to think about it. I never beat a child now because I have become aware of the dangers in beating and I am quite aware of the hate behind the beating.

At Summerhill we treat children as equals. By and large, we respect the individuality and personality of a child just as we would respect the individuality and personality of an adult, knowing that the child is different from an adult. We adults do not demand that adult Uncle Bill must clear his plate when he dislikes carrots, or that father must wash his hands before he sits down to a meal. By continually correcting children, we make them feel inferior. We injure their natural dignity. It is all a question of relative values. In heaven's name, what does it really matter if Tommy sits down to a meal with unwashed hands?

Children brought up under the wrong type of discipline live one lifelong lie. They never dare be themselves. They become slaves to established futile customs and manners. They accept their silly Sunday clothes without question. For the mainspring of discipline is fear of censure. Punishment from their playfellows does not involve fear. But when an adult punishes, fear comes automatically. For the adult is big and strong and awe-inspiring. Most important of all, he is a symbol of the feared father or feared mother.

For thirty-eight years, I have seen nasty, cheeky, hateful children come to the freedom of Summerhill. In every case, a gradual change took place. In time, these spoiled children have become happy, social, sincere, and friendly children.

The future of humanity rests with the new parents. If they ruin the life force in their children by arbitrary authority, crime and war and misery will go on flourishing. If they carry on in the footsteps of their disciplinary parents, they will lose the love of their children. For no one can love what he fears.

Neurosis begins with parental discipline—which is the very opposite of parental love. You cannot have a good humanity by treating it with hate and punishment and suppression. The only way is the way of love.

A loving environment, without parental discipline, will take care of most of the troubles of childhood. This is what I want parents to realize. If their children are given an environment of love and approval in the home, nastiness, hate, and destructiveness will never arise.

The Road to Happiness

Freud showed that every neurosis is founded on sex repression. I said, "I'll have a school in which there will be no sex repression." Freud said that the unconscious was infinitely more important and more powerful than the conscious. I said, "In my school we won't censure, punish, moralize. We will allow every child to live according to his deep impulses."

I slowly discovered that most of the Freudians did not understand or believe in freedom for children. They confused freedom with license. They had been treating children who had never had freedom to be themselves, and who had therefore developed no natural respect for the freedom of others. I am convinced that the Freudians founded their theory of child psychology on these warped children.

The Freudians found a great deal of anal eroticism among infants, but I have not found this to be true with self-regulated babies. The antisocial aggression the Freudians found in children does not seem to be there in self-regulated children.

I gradually learned that my territory was prophylaxis—not curing. It took me years to discover the full significance of this, to learn that it was freedom that was helping Summerhill problem children, not therapy. I find that my chief job is to sit still and approve of all the things that a child disapproves of in himself—that is, I try to break down the child's superimposed conscience, his self-hatred.

A new boy swears. I smile and say, "Carry on! Nothing bad about swearing." So with masturbation, lying, stealing, and other socially condemned activities.

Some time ago, I had a small boy who deluged me with questions: "What did you pay for that clock?" "What time is it?"

"When does the school term end?" He was full of anxiety and never heard any answer I gave him. I knew he was evading the big question that he wanted to have answered.

One day, he came to my room and asked a string of questions. I made no reply, and went on reading my book. After a dozen questions, I looked up casually and said, "What was that you asked? Where do babies come from?"

He got up, reddening. "I don't want to know where babies come from," he said, as he went out, slamming the door.

Ten minutes later he came back. "Where did you get your typewriter from? What's playing at the movie theater this week? How old are you? (*Pause.*) Well, damn it all, where *do* babies come from?"

I gave him the correct answer. He never came back to ask me any more questions.

Clearing away rubbish is never anything else but toil. Work of this kind is made tolerable only by the delight of seeing an unhappy child become happy and free.

The other side of the picture is the long, tiresome study of a child with no success forthcoming. One will work with a child for a year, and at the end of that year be overjoyed to think that the boy is cured of stealing. Then one day the boy relapses, and the teacher almost despairs. I have patted myself on the back about a particular pupil and then five minutes later have had a teacher rush in and say, "Tommy has been stealing again."

Yet psychology is somewhat like golf: you may go two hundred strokes on a round, you may swear and break your clubs—but on the next sunny morning, you will walk to the first tee with new hope in your heart.

If you tell a child any vital truth or if he confides his troubles to you, he forms a transference—that is, you get all the child's emotions showered on you. When I have cleared up a small child about birth and masturbation, the transference is especially strong. At one stage, it may even take the form of a negative transference, a hate transference. But with a normal child this negative phase does not last long, and the positive love transference soon follows. A child's transference dissolves easily. He soon forgets all about me, and his emotions go out to other children and to things. Since I am a father substitute, girls naturally develop a stronger transference to me than boys do, but I cannot say that a girl always develops a positive transference and a boy always develops a negative transference. On the contrary, I have had girls who showed quite a fierce hatred of me for a time.

At Summerhill, I used to be both teacher and psychologist. Then I slowly discovered that a man cannot play both these roles. I have had to give up being a psychiatrist, for most pupils cannot do much work with the man who is their father confessor. They become irritated and are always in much fear of my criticism. Moreover, if I praise the drawing of any one child, I evoke much jealousy among the other children. The psychic doctor should not really live in the school at all; the children should have no social interest in him.

All schools of psychology recognize the hypothesis of the unconscious, the principle that we all have buried wishes and loves and hates that we are not conscious of. Character is a combination of conscious behavior and unconscious behavior.

The housebreaking youth is conscious that he wants to acquire money or goods, but he does not know the deep motive that makes him choose this way of getting money instead of the social way of earning it. That motive is buried, and that is why moral lectures or punishments never cure him. Scoldings are heard only by his ears, and punishments are felt only by his body. But these preachments and punishments never penetrate to the unconscious motive which controls his behavior.

Because this is so, religion cannot reach a boy's unconscious through preachment. But if some night his curate went out stealing with him, that action would begin to dissolve the self-hatred responsible for the antisocial behavior. That sympathetic kinship would start the boy thinking in different terms. The cure of more than one young thief began when I joined him stealing our neighbor's hens or helped him rob the school's pocket-money drawer. Action touches the unconscious where words cannot. This is why love and approval will so often cure a child's problems. I do not say that love will cure a case of acute claustrophobia or a case of marked sadism; but generally, love will cure most young thieves and liars and destroyers. I have proved in action that freedom and the absence of moral discipline have cured many children whose future had appeared to be a life in prison.

True freedom practiced in community living, as in Summerhill, seems to do for the many what psychoanalysis does for the individual. It releases what is hidden. It is a breath of fresh air blowing through the soul to cleanse it of self-hatred and hatred of others.

The battle for youth is one with the gloves off. None of us can be neutral. We must take one side or the other: authority or freedom; discipline or self-government. No half measures will do. The situation is too urgent.

To be a free soul, happy in work, happy in friendship, and happy in love or to be a miserable bundle of conflicts, hating one's self and hating humanity—one or the other is the legacy that parents and teachers give to every child.

How can happiness be bestowed? My own answer is: Abolish authority. Let the child be himself. Don't push him around. Don't teach him. Don't lecture him. Don't elevate him. Don't force him to do anything. It may not be your answer. But if you reject my answer, it is incumbent on you to find a better one.

About the Author

William Ayers began teaching in 1965 in an experimental free school associated with the civil rights movement. He has been involved in community and adult education, prison education, and a variety of school reform projects and movements. He has taught preschool through graduate school, has lived in a residential home for "delinquent" youngsters, and has founded and directed three different alternative schools. His own children have been a major source for thinking and rethinking issues of teaching and learning. He is author of *The Good Preschool Teacher* (Teachers College Press, 1989), and *To Teach: The Journey of a Teacher, Second Edition* (Teachers College Press, 2001). Currently a Distinguished Professor of Education at the University of Illinois at Chicago, he lives with Bernardine Dohrn in Hyde Park, Chicago.